How to Decorate & Furnish Your Apartment on a Budget

How to **Decorate** & **Furnish** Your **Apartment** on a **Budget**

From Budgeting to Shopping,

Your Idea Source for Transforming

Your Apartment into a Beautiful Home

Lourdes Dumke

Prima Publishing

Published by Prima Publishing, Roseville, California. Member of the Crown Publishing Group, a division of Random House, Inc.

PRIMA PUBLISHING and colophon are trademarks of Random House, Inc., registered with the United States Patent and Trademark Office.

Interior and cover illustrations by Mary Rich.

Library of Congress Cataloging-in-Publication Data

Dumke, Lourdes.
   How to decorate & furnish your apartment on a budget: from budgeting to shopping, your idea source for transforming your apartment into a beautiful home / Lourdes Dumke
     p.   cm.
   Includes index.
   ISBN 0-7615-3247-1
   1. Apartments. 2. Interior decoration–Amaterus' manuals. I. Title
NK2195.A6. D86   2001
747'.88314--dc21   2001018519

02 03 04 05 BB 10 9 8 7 6 5 4 3 2
Printed in the United States of America
First Edition

Visit us online at www.primapublishing.com

To my children, Jillian and Mitchell,
and my husband, Keith.

Thanks for your unending supply of encouragement,
patience, and love.

Contents at a Glance

Contents

Acknowledgments

Thanks to my parents, sister, brother, and nieces for all your support over the years.

Thanks to Tim and Lisa Glover for reminding me to chase my dreams and for making me believe I have the power to make those dreams come true.

Thanks to Sharon Spalten for keeping me sane and centered in this crazy, off-balance world.

Thanks to the folks at the Suite 101 Internet community for publishing my budget decorating articles since 1999.

Introduction

You may live in a high-rise apartment in the center of a bustling urban area or in a quaint townhouse in a quiet suburb. It may be your first apartment, your fifth, or your fifteenth. You may be planning to live there just a few months, or you may be decidedly planted there for the foreseeable future. Anyway you look at it, your apartment is your home—shouldn't it be decorated to feel that way? Absolutely!

This book will help you furnish and decorate your apartment on a tight budget. If you're ready and willing, you'll have many options for creating a beautiful home environment while staying well within your budget, no matter what your decorating style may be. And don't worry if you don't think of yourself as the "creative type." Most of the ideas in this book are simple enough that even the artistically challenged can execute them with ease.

How I Got Started

"How did you think of that?" friends often ask, as they point out decorative accents and furnishings in my home. "Did you buy it that way?" is another one I hear, and "Are you an interior designer?" is one of my favorites. Well, it's time to fess up and set the record straight.

Like many wonderful things in life, I became a devoted budget decorator by accident. I am not a professionally trained interior decorator, nor am I a fine artist or a furniture designer. I'm a journalist who writes often about home- and garden-related topics. I'm also a suburban mom, an avid crafter, and a collector of low-cost antiques. (Okay, some people refer to me as a "junk lover," but I think my description is more kind.) I became a budget decorator because I had no choice if I wanted to have a beautifully decorated home. Necessity breeds innovation—and boy did I have *necessity!*

My pursuit for a charming yet inexpensively decorated home began more than a decade ago. I married at twenty-four, and my husband and I lived the comfortable lifestyle of yuppies in an Atlanta suburb. We filled our rooms with new furniture and accessories from places like Ethan Allen, Storehouse, Havertys, Macy's, and Pier 1 Imports. (All wonderful places to shop, by the way!) Then, at twenty-six, I had my first child. I had intended to return to my full-time job at a magazine publishing company after a six-week maternity leave. I wasn't ready to give up my career yet, so I assumed I'd just insert a new baby into the picture and life would continue as it had before my unexpected pregnancy.

But things didn't turn out quite the way I'd planned. I quickly realized I wanted to spend more time with my new baby, and I was simply not ready to go back to work full time. I resigned from my job and became a full-time mother.

When I gave up my job, I gained a lot of happiness, but I lost my full-time salary. Some of the "luxuries" in my life had to go, and decorating was one of the first budgets to be sliced. (Actually, *eliminated* is more accurate.) This was no problem for a while. Because most of our furnishings and accessories were new, I was quite pleased with my home and desired very little. But after a few years, I began to get antsy. I wanted to make some changes. Since I could not afford to purchase many new items for my home, I had to think creatively. So to begin, I purchased some stencils and transformed my living room by painting an ivy border along the chair rail. The total cost for the stencils and paint was less than $15. I was amazed at how much I could do while spending so little. And that's about the time I was bitten by the budget decorating bug.

Next, a neighbor taught me how to decorate baskets with scraps of fabric and fabric stiffening liquid. I decorated several baskets to hold everything from magazines to toys to toiletries. I combed the clearance section of department stores for discounted sheets and pillowcases and made my own window treatments—and I didn't even sew at the time. I made a set of formal-looking curtains for my dining room using two irregular full-size flat sheets, a fleur-de-lis stencil, and a little gold paint. The total cost of the project: less than $10 per window.

Budget decorating became a hobby for me, and today, more than a decade later, I am constantly discovering creative ways to decorate my home for little or no money. In 1999, I signed on as the budget decorating contributing editor for the Suite 101 community on the Internet. I began to share my ideas with Internet users from all over the world, and they shared their ideas with me. I learned that I was far from alone in my ceaseless pursuit to decorate on a tight budget. Budget decorating is a fun, incredibly rewarding hobby. Best of all, you will reap the benefits of this hobby each day as you enjoy your comfortable, wonderfully decorated home space.

In Chapter 1, you will learn about getting organized, creating a decorating notebook, and taking other steps as you begin your adventure of decorating your entire apartment on a modest budget.

Finding the Right Apartment

If you're currently searching for the perfect place to call home, begin your search by trying the following suggestions:

❖ Drive around town and jot down the names of apartment complexes that appeal to you.

❖ Ask friends and coworkers about where they live and whether they like it.

❖ Contact an apartment finder service in your area (check your local phone book).

❖ Visit Internet sites established to aid in apartment searches. Apartments.com (www.apartments.com) has a searchable database, Spectrum Apartment Search (www.apartmentsearch.com) offers search capabilities and "City Guides" with information on U.S. cities, and Apartment Guide.com (www.apartmentguide.com) has a nifty "Shop & Compare" feature.

Once you've found a place you like, walk or drive by at different times of day and observe the surroundings. Think about what you see—are children running around playing? Is this something you would enjoy, or would you prefer a quieter, adult-only complex? Are the grounds well kept, and are the general areas pleasant to look at and spend time in? Close your eyes and picture an apartment and a community that make you comfortable and happy. Then determine whether you have that feeling again when you are visiting some of the apartments you are considering for your new home.

It's also a good idea to test your morning and evening commutes at the exact times of day you will be making those commutes. I once almost turned down a lovely apartment because the location was going to add about eight miles to my commute to work. But after a morning and evening test run, I was completely turned around. I discovered several low-traffic shortcuts from this apartment that actually sliced my prior commute time nearly in half! You just never know, so don't take chances. Make that drive!

Remember That Apartment?

Apartment hunting can be a daunting proposition. By the time you've seen a few places, they can begin to blend together into one big blur of rooms in your mind. It can be difficult to remember the features you liked or disliked in the first or second apartment by the time you reach the sixth.

To keep your head clear and the details straight, take a notebook with you when you hunt for your apartment, and jot down a few identifiers for each one you visit. Also record the most attractive features, as well as the most unattractive, and anything else that may impact your decision. For example, your notes could read as follows:

Regal Road Apartment
- Very large rooms
- Nice view of the pond from living room
- Very small deck with no privacy
- Odd green paint in kitchen

If you're absolutely determined to find the perfect apartment, you could take along a camera or video camera. (Be sure to ask the leasing agent's or landlord's permission before you photograph or videotape the space.) Instant cameras work great, since you can snap the photo and jot down notes on the photo borders. And while you're there, don't forget to stop a few residents and ask them how they like living there. As far as the leasing agent goes, be sure to take lots of questions with you so you won't have surprises *after* you sign the lease. Your questions may include pet policies, deposit amount, penalties for breaking a lease, and whether any utilities are covered by your rent payment.

Once you've selected an apartment, you can begin to plan your decorating pursuits before you move in. Buy some decorating magazines and cut out pictures that appeal to you. Have a garage sale or donate items you do not need or that no longer suit your taste. I dragged several items from apartment to apartment for years, even though I did not want or need them anymore. The day I sold them all in a yard sale was very freeing—give it a try!

How to Use This Book

This book is designed to be a source of inspiration and a workbook for you to use as you decorate your apartment. In chapter 1 and the Appendix, you'll find several worksheets and checklists designed to help you work through the decorating process. I encourage you to photocopy these worksheets, fill them out, and keep them in your decorating notebook. (More about creating a decorating notebook in chapter 1 and the Appendix.)

Now, let the budget decorating adventure begin!

How to Decorate & Furnish Your Apartment on a Budget

chapter **1**

Getting Started

It's time to begin, and there's much work to do! When you stand looking at your apartment walls—whether it's a place you've just moved into or one where you've lived for a while—you will find that temptation is everywhere.

So what *should* you do? Resist that urge, that's what. As enticing as a blank wall may be, as irresistible as an empty corner may seem, don't begin decorating yet. Before you hang a single piece of artwork or purchase a single piece of furniture, you need to stop, think, and plan. And the way to begin is by answering the following question: "What in the world do I really want to accomplish here?"

Determining Your Decorating Goals

I once lived in a beautiful, two-story, brick townhouse near downtown Atlanta. The thirty-year-old building had been painstakingly renovated just before I moved in, and it was a truly charming place. My unit featured large rooms, new appliances, attractive architectural details, fresh paint, and new carpeting.

Yet, despite all its lovely features, I simply could not make this apartment *work*. No matter what I did, no matter which room I was in, something always felt not quite right. Even the day-to-day aspects of living often seemed tough there. The television set was too far away from the couch, so watching the evening news was difficult from the only comfortable spot in the room. The breakfast dinette was crammed into an uncomfortable corner of the kitchen and was nearly impossible to reach, so I usually ate my first meal of the day standing up. The list of what seemed "wrong" went on and on—the apartment just wasn't set up for what I would call comfortable living, and I became more aware of this as the months passed.

My discomfort, however, should not have come as a big surprise to me. I had moved into this townhouse unexpectedly when my previous apartment flooded. I was forced to relocate very quickly and found the women living in the townhouse through a mutual friend. I met them and moved in all in the course of a week, and I moved my belongings into the new place in a near frenzy since my flooded apartment was uninhabitable.

Most of the rooms were completely furnished and accessorized by the time I moved into the townhouse. I inserted my meager truckload of belongings into my bedroom, and this room became where I lived most of my life. When I was home, I was in my bedroom. I wasn't sure what exactly was wrong with the rest of the apartment, but I did know it felt cold and uninviting, and I felt very unattached to this place I called home.

A New Beginning

No surprise, I was eager to move out when my six-month lease expired. One of my roommates and I found another apartment in the same area. But this time, everything was different. We were excited about this new place, although it was not nearly as physically attractive as the townhouse. Our new apartment's carpeting was brown and faded badly in some areas, the kitchen was too small and dark, and the deck offered no privacy. But you know what? I loved this place! The reason was simple: I decorated it with specific goals and in a style that suited me.

You may be thinking, "Oh, that must have required lots of money," but that's not the case. To say that I was flat broke at the time is an understatement. I was twenty-three years old and living from paycheck to paycheck. I was able to pay my bills but had little left over (most months, I had nothing left over) for decorating. So, why did this new place work so well, when the other one didn't? I believe my new apartment worked well *because* the other one did not. I walked away from the townhouse having learned a few lessons about furniture placement and flow. Basically, I learned what I did not want to do because I'd been so uncomfortable in my last place.

What a Difference a Goal Makes

When I stood looking at my empty new apartment, I began to develop my goals by asking myself, "What do I want to accomplish in this room?" In the living room, comfort was paramount. In the kitchen, I opted for efficiency. I wanted my bathroom to be a cheerful place that helped put me in a good mood, because, not being a morning person, I needed all the help I could get. My bedroom needed to be clean, simple, and streamlined, because I didn't have the time or desire to dust often or take care of lots of trinkets and unnecessary accessories. I also suffered from frequent bouts with insomnia, so I wanted my bedroom to be a calming, peaceful place in hopes that it would help ease me into sleep each night.

For the first few weeks, I poured over the Sunday newspaper's sale sections and located the best white sales in town. I asked friends and coworkers about where they shopped and located discount stores I never even knew existed, though some were very close to my home. I hit many of these places on my lunch hour during the week, and I spent Saturday mornings at yard sales. I visited my mother's home and convinced her to part with a few lovely pieces of furniture she really didn't have the space for anyway. I arranged my furniture and accessories with care. When we ran out of money, my roommate and I got creative. One day, as we faced a bare wall sporting nothing more than an unadorned twig wreath, we labored over how to dress it up. My roommate disappeared for a moment and returned with a bouquet of silk flowers she had carried as a bridesmaid in a friend's wedding. She fastened it to the inside lower part of the wreath and voilà!—a colorful new wall hanging was born.

Another dilemma surfaced as we searched for a spot for our television set. We did not own end tables or an entertainment unit, and the television set was far too small to sit on the floor. Then I remembered that I did have a very inexpensive drafting table that I had dragged along with me from apartment to apartment since college. I never needed to use it for its original purpose again, but I'd held onto it and kept it in a closet all this time. We dragged it out, covered it with a plain flat sheet and a lace topper, and our television set had a wonderful new place to rest (see example in illustration 1-A).

The result of all my intentional, goal-minded efforts was an apartment I was proud to call home for a year. I continued to borrow, create, and recycle home furnishings, having learned a valuable lesson from what did not work in my previous home. I learned to decorate with a goal, and it made all the difference in the world.

Illustration 1-A. Improvised television stand.

So, What's Important to You?

Stop and think for a moment about the way you live and, more important, the way you *want* to live. What type of environment appeals to you? Is comfort high on your list? Do you yearn for a light, airy environment, or do you thrive on intense colors? Do you want your apartment to embrace you warmly and peacefully when you arrive home each day, or do you want it to help energize you when you walk through your door?

The questions in figure 1.1 will help you begin to determine your decorating goals. (See an example of a completed Decorating Goals Questionnaire in figure 1.2.)

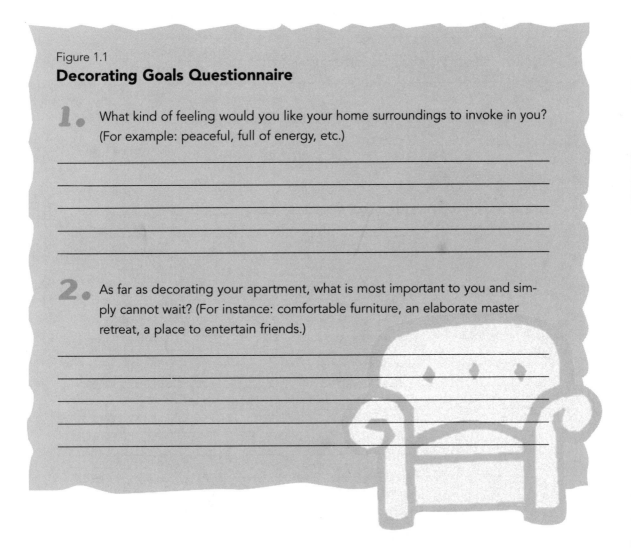

Figure 1.1
Decorating Goals Questionnaire

1. What kind of feeling would you like your home surroundings to invoke in you? (For example: peaceful, full of energy, etc.)

_____

_____

_____

_____

_____

2. As far as decorating your apartment, what is most important to you and simply cannot wait? (For instance: comfortable furniture, an elaborate master retreat, a place to entertain friends.)

_____

_____

_____

_____

_____

3. Can you think of decorating elements you would like to have eventually but can wait? (For instance: new artwork on the walls, more Contemporary accessories.)

_____

_____

_____

_____

_____

_____

_____

4. Describe your idea of how the perfect apartment would look.

_____

_____

_____

_____

_____

_____

_____

5. Using the information you've just supplied, write your own decorating goals statement.

_____

_____

_____

_____

_____

Figure 1.2
Completed Questionnaire Sample

1. What kind of feeling would you like your home surroundings to invoke in you?

I would like my home to help me ease slowly into the evening and help me feel calm and peaceful at the end of a stressful day.

2. As far as decorating your apartment, what is most important to you and simply cannot wait?

I must have comfortable furniture in the living room and a home office area where I can pay bills and occasionally work at home.

3. Can you think of decorating elements you would like to have eventually but can wait?

I do not feel the immediate need to have a guest bed, since I rarely have overnight guests. I also do not need a large dining area, since I do not entertain large groups very often.

4. Describe your idea of how the perfect apartment would look.

My perfect apartment would be cozy and homey and filled with my favorite things. I could display my collections for visitors to see, but they would be neat and orderly. I do not like a lot of knickknacks that have no purpose.

5. Using the information you've just supplied, write your own decorating goals statement.

I would like to create an apartment home that incorporates my love of collectibles and country decor, with an orderly way to display my collections, a comfortable living room, and a small home office area.

Stay True to Your Goals

Now that you've completed your decorating goals statement, you have taken the first step toward decorating your apartment to be the home of your dreams—good work! It's very important to remember this statement as you begin to make your decisions, particularly about what you purchase and which areas you tackle first. Refer to this statement often. The objective is to make sure that *every decorating decision you make supports your final goals*. This may take some practice and discipline to master, but it's essential if you plan to stick to your budget. Without dedication to a solid goal, you may end up with a lot of items you never needed, and you may never get around to purchasing the items you really want.

For instance, let's say you are setting out for a Saturday morning of cruising yard sales to hunt for treasures. Before you depart, review your goals. Using figure 1.2 as our example, your main goal for a yard sale excursion would be to search out items such as the following: display shelves for collectibles, a home office desk and chair, and a comfortable sofa for your living room. As tempting as it may be, muster the willpower to pass up an adorable, barely used armoire priced at just $20. If you really need a home office desk, chances are you will regret the armoire purchase after you get home and realize you have nowhere to work on your telecommuting days.

Also use your decorating goals statement to create shopping lists. But don't wait until you're heading off to a flea market, discount store, or yard sale to create your list! As soon as you clearly have in mind what you need, create a master list and keep it with you at all times—in your purse, wallet, car, or other convenient location. Having this list handy is vital because you might just see an estate sale while you're running errands on your lunch hour or stumble across a flea market on your way to a friend's house. Keeping this list available will help you stay on track and on budget when bargains unexpectedly appear.

Living Your Style

I have some friends whose soft Contemporary style I simply love. Whenever they purchase new furniture, an accessory, or a piece of art, it always looks perfect in their space. Their home is full of sets—coordinated art prints, full sets of matching furniture, things like that. The result is a wonderfully pulled-together look. (And it makes buying them gifts very easy!)

My style is very different from theirs. My home is full of wood furniture with peeling paint, antiques, quilts, and folk art. In contrast to my very stylish friends, my home isn't full of matched sets of furniture or coordinated accessories. I have a Picasso print hanging under a battered old piece of architectural salvage. My clean-lined, Mission-style couch is decorated with a quilt and floral-print pillows. And in front of my well-worn, hundred-year-old mantel (which is just leaning up against a wall, no fireplace in sight), I have a sleek, modern-flavored orchid secured into a white porcelain vase.

At first glance, it may seem that my friends and I live at opposite ends of the decorating spectrum—they with their perfectly matched sets, me with my mishmash of styles, textures, and colors. But if you look beyond the obvious—beyond the differences— you'll see that we're actually very similar in the way we decorate. We are all people who know what we like and we stick to it.

Even if you know what you like and what you don't like, try to remember that decorating style preferences change over the years. In the mid-1980s, I loved to decorate with Modern style. I had plenty of black, white, and red in my apartment, and geometric shapes adorned the art on the walls and even my bedroom's comforter and sheets. In the early 1990s, I was more partial to a Traditional look. A few years ago, I briefly flirted with the clean lines and dark woods of Mission style. Now, I've made my home into a Cottage-style haven. Looking back, I couldn't have predicted where my decorating taste would eventually end up. The only real constant seems to be that every five years or so, my style changes. I don't always experience a drastic change, but, even from year to year, my preferences are always evolving.

So what's your style? See the style chart provided in figure 1.3 to learn more about some of the most popular decorating styles.

Figure 1.3

STYLE CHART

COUNTRY: You enjoy warm and cozy surroundings. Floral fabrics, slipcovers, wicker, and quilts may be found in your home, along with an old pie safe in the kitchen and big baskets (as storage for just about anything) in your living room.

CONTEMPORARY: This style means contemporary at this moment, so it changes often. This style is often sleek and simple, and it may be influenced by things such as technology.

ECLECTIC: If you like Eclectic decorating, you probably have a mix of styles-such as Country, Southwestern, and Contemporary, all in one room. This style can be fun, interesting, and energetic.

TRADITIONAL: If a chintz sofa and tailored silk curtains please you, you're probably traditional at heart. This style is timeless and often includes rich colors.

MODERN: Often confused with Contemporary, but Modern does not change with the times—it is constant. Modern style includes clean lines and an emphasis on function.

Working With Your Budget

Your decorating goals statement will help you create a very important document: your budget sheet. Like other types of budgets, your decorating budget will help you direct your efforts and dollars into the right areas.

Begin by compiling a list of your priority items for decorating your apartment. List the items you feel you need to purchase, in the order of their importance to you. Your list may include items such as a sofa, a coffee table, storage for a book collection, living room art, and bathroom accessories.

Now complete your list of priorities on the lines below. Be as specific as possible:

_____

_____

_____

_____

_____

_____

_____

_____

_____

_____

_____

_____

_____

_____

_____

_____

_____

Examine your list carefully. Now answer the following questions:

- ❖ Do all of these items need to be purchased new?

- ❖ Are there any items on the list you may be able to borrow or trade?

- ❖ Do your parents, grandparents, or other family members have attics or basements full of furnishings that are perfectly usable, or at least items that could be recycled into unique pieces?

Now return to your list and mark the items that you feel must be purchased new. Some items—such as baby cribs—should be purchased new (or relatively new) to ensure that they meet current safety standards. Other items, such as mattresses, may also be preferable if purchased new or slightly used. But many decorative elements, particularly accessories, can easily be located at flea markets, garage sales, and consignment shops for a fraction of what they would cost in a retail store. In addition, if you're willing to purchase secondhand items, you may be able to have items you might not have if you opted for new furnishings only.

Now return to your list and mark all the items you would like to purchase new with an *N*. Remember that just because you hope to find some secondhand items doesn't mean you have to pass up new ones if you find a great bargain. This list is simply a guide to help you stay on track and spend your money wisely.

With your list of priorities now complete, it's time to begin work on your decorating budget worksheet. The estimates provided on the sample worksheet (figure 1.4) represent a high/low price range. The low end of the range indicates a secondhand find or item purchased from a discount store, and the high end indicates the cost for that item if purchased new at a retail store. (Remember: Selecting many of the higher-end items may not fit into your budget.)

In addition to the worksheet provided for your use, figure 1.5 (a, b, and c) is offered as a complete budget sample for three budgets: $500, $1,000, and $5,000. Each sample includes a brief description of items chosen for each category.

Figure 1.4

Your Decorating Budget Worksheet

Living Room	*Price Range*	
Sofa	$50–1,000	_____
Living room chairs (2)	$50–1,000	_____
Stereo	$80–700	_____
Television set	$100–1,000	_____
Coffee table	$15–500	_____
Entertainment unit	$50–1,000	_____
Bookcase	$50–500	_____
Area rug	$20–500	_____
Artwork/accessories	$10–1,000	_____
Window treatments (2)	$15–200	_____
Lamps (2)	$20–200	_____

Home Office Area		
Computer & printer	$700–2,000	_____
Desk & drawer unit	$75–800	_____
Chair	$20–300	_____
Bookshelf	$30–800	_____
Bulletin board	$10–50	_____
Supplies storage	$5–150	_____
Lamp	$10–100	_____
Trash can	$10–25	_____
Cordless phone	$20–150	_____

Filing cabinet	$20–100	_____
Artwork/accessories	$10–1,000	_____
Window treatment	$15–100	_____

Kitchen

Dining table & chairs (4)	$50–800	_____
Trash can	$10–25	_____
Canister set	$5–50	_____
Clock	$5–80	_____
Dish rack	$10–50	_____
Kitchen towels	$10–30	_____
China	$20–200	_____
Cutlery	$20–150	_____
Cookware	$40–200	_____
Cordless phone	$20–150	_____
Small window treatment	$15–50	_____
Artwork/accessories	$10–1,000	_____

Bedroom

Bed	$50–400	_____
Chair	$20–350	_____
Dresser	$30–500	_____
Nightstands (2)	$20–400	_____
Area rug	$20–500	_____
Mirror	$10–200	_____
Lamp	$10–100	_____
Bedspread/shams	$20–200	_____
Sheets & pillowcases	$15–60	_____
Shoe organizer	$20–50	_____
Closet organizer	$15–250	_____

Artwork/accessories	$10–1,000	_____
Window treatment (2)	$15–100	_____
Bathroom		
Bathroom rug	$10–25	_____
Shower curtain & hooks	$10–50	_____
Trash can	$10–25	_____
Small window treatment	$7–50	_____
Clothes hamper	$10–40	_____
Artwork/accessories	$10–1,000	_____
Balcony		
Gas grill	$100–300	_____
Patio furniture set	$30–350	_____
Plants	$10–50	_____

Completed Budget Samples

I have created the following completed budget samples using prices collected in the fall of 2000 from sales fliers, Internet sites, catalogs, and visits to flea markets, yard sales, and particular stores. (Some of the prices indicate items that were on sale at that time.)

The prices in your area for the same products may vary widely. These samples are not intended to represent current prices; they are simply a guide you may use in creating your own budget. The asterisk (*) denotes items that I would consider a *splurge*–items that may be purchased less expensively but would be items high on the priority list for whatever reason. Remember: It's okay to splurge if you really want an item and can make up the difference by spending less on items that aren't as important to you.

The examples in figures 1.5a, 1.5b, and 1.5c cover items that could be used for a one-bedroom, one-bathroom apartment with a dining room/living room combination, a home office area, and a balcony.

Figure 1.5a
$5,000 Budget

Area/Items	Amount Spent	Item Chosen
Living Room		
Sofa	$200	From garage sale. New slipcover added. (Fabric purchased on sale at fabric store and sewn by a friend.)
Living room chairs (2)	$100	On clearance at furniture outlet store
Stereo w/3 CD changer	$90	On sale at Kmart
Television set, 19-inch	$140	On sale at Wal-Mart
Coffee table	$0	A trunk from my grandma's attic. (Grandma was happy to get it out of her way.) Also serves as storage for arts and crafts supplies.
Entertainment unit	$80	On sale at Kmart
Bookcase for book collection	$60	Folding bookcase from Bed, Bath & Beyond
Area rug, 4' × 6'	$210	*From Sundance catalog
Artwork/accessories	$350	Nephew's artwork matted & framed; original folk art painting from eBay; coat rack from garage sale, painted; frames for family photos from discount store; 4 candles from discount store; fireplace screen made from old iron gate from junk shop; 2 baskets from Pier 1 Imports, on sale; 1 sap bucket for holding flowers from antique fair; and from Pottery Barn: *crown moulding ledges and sconces (2)

Window treatments (2)	$25	Full sheets (irregular, on sale at discount store), adorned with stencil & paint, and curtain rods
Lamps (2)	$50	Garage sale finds, with bases painted & decorative beads (from Motherbeads.com) added

Home Office Area

Computer & printer	$1,200	From Costco, includes mail-in rebates
Desk & drawer unit	$150	From IKEA's (U.S) Web site (used to hold printer)
Chair	$35	Computer chair from company's going-out-of-business sale
Bookshelf	$75	* Antique bookshelf from an estate sale
Bulletin board	$25	From Office Depot; ribbon trim added for interest
Supplies storage	$50	Five old suitcases stacked, $10 each at flea market
Lamp	$20	From discount store, on clearance
Trash can	$15	Large wicker basket (with lid), from discount wicker warehouse
Cordless phone	$20	From Kmart, on sale
Filing cabinet	$15	Used, from company's going-out-of-business sale
Artwork/accessories	$200	* Wall organizer from Pottery Barn $79; 3 matching framed botanical prints, from consignment shop
Window treatment	$25	Roller shade, decorated with leftover fabric and buttons

Kitchen

Dining table & chairs (4)	$90	From Kmart, on sale
Trash can	$10	From discount store
Canister set	$15	Ball jars, picked up at yard sale
Clock	$70	* From Restoration Hardware catalog.
Dish rack	$13	From Bed, Bath & Beyond's Web site
Kitchen towels	$10	Set of 5 towels from Bed, Bath & Beyond's Web site

China set	$20	From Target, 24-piece set
Cutlery	$25	From Target, 20-piece set
Cookware	$67	From Target
Cordless phone	$20	From Kmart, on sale
Small window treatment	$12	Four embroidered cloth napkins (from flea market) folded over a rod to create a valance
Artwork/accessories	$100	Spice rack from Grandma's attic; 2 framed prints of vegetables from yard sale; a cutting board table on clearance at discount store; a twig wreath adorned with silk flowers and vines, made with materials from craft supply store

Bedroom

Bed	$200	Mattress set on sale from discount furniture outlet. Headboard created with picket fencing from Home Depot ($20), cut and painted.
Chair	$30	A well-worn but very solid chair with floral print, from country rummage shop. (And they threw in a free matching foot stool.) Tossed a quilt over it, courtesy of Grandma.
Dresser	$80	* Antique wooden dresser with 4 drawers, missing knobs and sporting a few scratches. Fixed scratches with shoe polish and purchased new knobs.
Nightstands (2)	$30	Two wooden crates from crafts store, painted
Area rug	$70	From Kmart
Mirror	$25	Large mirror from estate sale. Had a beautiful frame that was unfortunately painted a gaudy gold. Sanded down and whitewashed it with watered-down primer for a Cottage look.
Lamp	$20	From yard sale, shade replaced
Bedspread & shams	$125	Quilt and shams from The Company Store catalog
Sheets & pillowcases	$20	Queen set from Steinmart, on sale

Shoe organizer	$15	From Home Depot
Closet organizer	$48	10' closet organizer from Home Depot
Artwork/accessories	$100	Art book purchased at used-book store, pages removed and framed; 4 antique dishes, purchased at flea market
Window treatments (2)	$14	Miniblinds from Home Depot

Bathroom

Bathroom rug	$14	From Kmart's Martha Stewart Everyday collection
Vinyl shower curtain & hooks	$13	From Kmart's Martha Stewart Everyday collection
Trash can	$10	From discount store
Small window treatment	$7	Miniblinds from Home Depot
Clothes hamper	$20	Large wicker basket, from discount wicker warehouse
Towels	$28	Set of 4 washcloths, 4 hand towels, and 2 bath towels from discount store
Artwork/accessories	$60	Two candles from Garden Ridge; old Coca-Cola crate hung on the wall as a shelf; 2 framed prints from yard sale

Balcony

Gas grill	$120	Grill from Home Depot
Patio furniture set	$40	Used set, found at flea market
Plants	$30	Potted plants from school fund-raising sale

Total cost: $4,706.00

Figure 1.5b

$1,000 Budget

Area/Items	Amount Spent	Item Chosen
Living Room		
Sofa & loveseat set	$150	Set from flea market
Bookcases	$60	Two bookcases from Wal-Mart
Coffee table	$0	Hand-me-down coffee table from sister who recently purchased a new one
Artwork/accessories	$75	Three small framed prints and assorted candles from Garden Ridge
Lamps (1)	$20	Torchère floor lamp from Bed, Bath & Beyond
Window treatment	$14	Two miniblinds from Home Depot
Home Office Area		
Desk & drawer unit	$79	Desk from IKEA's (U.S) Web site
Computer chair	$25	Used chair from flea market
Bulletin board	$25	From Office Depot, painted with two coordinating colors, hung from a decorative ribbon
Supplies storage	$20	Locker unit from school demolition sale
Lamp	$10	Desk lamp from Bed, Bath & Beyond
Trash can	$10	From discount store
Filing cabinet	$40	From Wal-Mart
Artwork/accessories	$20	Two frames for artwork, painted by talented teenage neighbor
Window treatment	$7	Miniblinds from Home Depot
Kitchen		
Dining table & chairs (4)	$90	Dining set from Kmart, on sale
Trash can	$10	Trash can from discount store

Small window treatment	$7	Miniblinds from Home Depot
Artwork/Accessories	$0	Tole trays from Mom's antique collection (Mom allowing an indefinite "borrow")

Bedroom

Bed	$0	Gift from aunt, who moved to a retirement community and did not have space for it
Dresser	$70	Unfinished wood dresser, stained
Nightstands (2)	$20	Two old wood chairs from flea market, painted vivid colors with latex paint
Lamp	$20	From yard sale, shade replaced
Bedspread & shams	$50	"Bed in a bag" complete set from Wal-Mart
Artwork/accessories	$50	Mirror from discount store, two prints from yard sale, candles
Window treatments (2)	$14	Miniblinds from Home Depot

Bathroom

Bathroom rug	$14	From Target
Vinyl shower curtain & hooks	$8	A vinyl liner paired with an heirloom tablecloth (gift)
Trash can	$10	From a discount store
Small window treatment	$7	Miniblinds from Home Depot
Artwork/accessories	$15	Wreath received as Christmas gift, with dried flowers added and holiday decorations removed

Balcony

Adirondack chairs	$40.	Plastic, from decorating store

Total cost: $980.00

Figure 1.5c

$500 Budget

Area/Items	Amount Spent	Item Chosen
Living Room		
Sofa & chair	$60	Hand-me-down sofa & chair; sofa cover sewn with discounted fabric
Bookcase	$30	From Wal-Mart; holds TV, stereo, and books
Artwork/accessories	$20	Family photos, frames from discount store
Lamp	$15	Garage sale find, embellished with paint, rubber stamps, and tassels
Home Office Area		
Desk	$59	Computer table from IKEA's (U.S) Web site
Chair	$15	Computer chair from yard sale
Supplies storage	$10	Large wicker baskets from discount wicker warehouse (stashed in closet)
Filing cabinet	$15	Used, from company's going-out-of-business sale, painted with leftover latex paint
Kitchen		
Dining table & chairs (4)	$62	Heavy plastic bistro set from discount store
Trash can	$10	From discount store Web site
Artwork/accessories	$7	Vegetables print from yard sale
Bedroom		
Bed	$0	Donated by Grandma
Chair	$15	Inflatable, from discount store
Dresser	$20	From yard sale, painted white and sanded for "distressed" look

Nightstands (2)	$24	Two small wooden shelves from crafts store, painted and hung on each side of bed
Lamp	$5	From yard sale, old family photos decoupaged on for interest and to cover faded shade
Bedspread & shams	$40	"Bed in a bag" set from linen store
Artwork/accessories	$15	Twig wreath adorned with old postcards and photos

Bathroom

Bathroom rug	$14	From Kmart
Shower curtain & hooks	$13	Vinyl, from Kmart
Trash can	$10	From discount store
Artwork/accessories	$15	Framed greeting cards

Balcony

| Chairs | $20 | Plastic Adirondack chair & small table |

Total cost: $494.00

If you're not quite sure what items you'll need, check figure 1.6 for furniture suggestions and figure 1.7 for accessory suggestions.

Figure 1.6
Furniture by Room

Living Room/Home Office	Bedroom	Kitchen	Bathroom
Sofa	Bed	Dining table	Shelving unit
Loveseat	Dresser	Chairs	Table
Coffee table	Chairs	Cutting block table	
Entertainment unit	Vanity	Step stool	
Bookshelves	Bookshelves	Bar stools	
Stereo	Nightstands		
Television	Desk		
Tables	Trunk/chest		
Desk			
Chair			
Computer			
Filing cabinet			
Ottoman			

Figure 1.7
Accessories by Room

Living Room/Home Office	Bedroom	Kitchen	Bathroom
Photos	Photos	Photos	Photos
Art	Art	Pot rack	Rugs
Area rug	Candles	Centerpiece	Hamper
Desk & chair	Lamps	Dish rack	Shower curtain
Coat rack	Closet organizer	Spice rack	Towel rack

Umbrella stand	Storage	Rug	Shelving
Office supplies storage	Lamp	Towels	
Books	Storage	Storage	
Candles			
Lamps			
Fireplace accessories			
Storage			

Getting Organized

Getting organized is more than just a great idea—it's practically a national obsession. Many books about organizing have been published over the last few years, and stores that sell nothing but organizing aides have popped up all over the country. Add to that the countless magazines, newsletters, and Web sites dedicated to the subject, and you have a bona fide organizing trend on your hands. So, you may be wondering, how exactly did we get to the point where we need all this help organizing our things and our lives? How did we even get so disorganized in the first place? For me, it happened gradually and in direct proportion to my age and career success. As a young, single woman, I felt very organized most of the time. I could always locate my address book, my favorite shoes, and my umbrella. After I started a family, however, things got more complicated. I added toys, children's clothing, and a husband's belongings to the mix, and suddenly I felt overwhelmed by the things around me. There came a time when I had to seek help or drown in my "stuff." Luckily, plenty of information was out there for me when that time came.

The Decorating/Organizing Link

So, what does all this have to do with decorating your apartment? Well, plenty, actually. Getting organized is a very important step in the decorating process. Until you have sorted through all your belongings and achieved a level of order, it's very difficult to know what you need to purchase for your decorating efforts.

But why is getting organized so important? Think of it this way: Have you ever gone to the grocery store and forgotten the one item you really needed, like a loaf of bread? And on that same trip to the store, did you manage to pick up a jar of mayonnaise, only to realize when you arrived home that you still have three unopened jars in your refrigerator? (If you have, you're certainly not alone!) Now, think of the same example in terms of furniture and accessories. You may never bring home a complete new bedroom set by accident when you set out to buy a dinette. But you may, for instance, find yourself buying yet another piece of Depression glass, even though what you really need is a new shelf to hold the glass collection you already have. If you have an extremely tight budget, you must know exactly what you have and what you need to purchase, borrow, or even make.

Of course, if you're moving to a new apartment, getting organized has even greater advantages. If you spend some time organizing your belongings and you throw out, give away, or otherwise clean out six boxes full of things, that's six fewer boxes you'll have to pack up, move, and unpack when you arrive at your new place. There's no reason to move something you don't want from home to home year after year.

For some people, getting organized can seem like a scary, overwhelming task. But it doesn't have to be. Just try to remember the following tips:

- ☉ **Start small.** If you have lots of stuff and the thought of organizing it all makes you feel like you're hyperventilating, slow down. Rather than approaching the task of organizing as one huge project, break it down into several smaller projects. When you begin, tackle a single closet or room. When you have completed this first step, cross it off your list. Set aside another day to organize another small area, and continue until you have completed your entire apartment. The key is to build up your momentum and to allow your successes to inspire you to organize even further. Taking on too much, like trying to tackle your entire apartment in one afternoon, can be overwhelming and tiring. Starting out this way can also lead you to give up before you get very far, because it simply feels like too much work and the rewards are too far out of your reach.

◎ **Box it up.** As you organize, keep several boxes on hand. Separate your items into several piles, such as items you *must keep*, items you'd *like to donate*, and a *"limbo"* box for items you don't really need but can't seem to give up. Record the current date on it and stash the limbo box in a place that's out of sight and out of mind, if you can. If you haven't opened the box six months or a year from now to retrieve an item, pitch it.

◎ **Maintain it.** Getting organized may be difficult, but it's staying organized that's really tough, according to Atlanta-area professional organizer, Peggy Duncan. Duncan says maintaining organization is all about making choices—every time you finish using an item, you must decide whether to put it back where it belongs. For more of Duncan's organizing tips, see "Tips for Organizing Success" sidebar on page 28.

Tips for Organizing Success

If clutter has taken over your space, and you've made up your mind to do something about it, you'll need a plan of action. But if the mere thought of tackling the mounds of clothes, papers, old food boxes, and magazines sends you screaming, you might need some creative motivation to get you going.

Peggy Duncan, an Atlanta-based professional organizer, offers these five tips:

1. **Try throwing a small party.** Invite your future in-laws, a childhood rival, your mom, or anyone else you want to impress. Set a date for the party, and you'll be ready to develop your plan.

2. **Visualize your space, and sketch some possible layouts.** Create places or "stations" for each of your activities. You'll need somewhere to work or study, somewhere to eat, somewhere to entertain, and somewhere to sleep.

3. **Once you've figured out the layout, it's time to deal with that mess.** Get a few large trash bags and attack one pile at a time. Finish one pile before moving on to another one, and stop when you feel tired. Sort through the piles and separate what you need to keep, give away, return, or store. When sorting your clothes, remember that if you didn't wear it last year, you probably won't wear it this year. And don't mix in clothes that need repair or cleaning.

4. **Once this process is over, you should only be dealing with the things you decided to keep.** You'll have to find a place for everything, and get in the habit of keeping everything in its place. Keep everything near its point of use, with like items together, and make sure it's convenient to put items back where they belong. To make this work, buy furniture and storage devices that have lots of drawers. Create extra space with storage racks that fit on doors, and don't forget about wall space and the space under your bed. An oversized trunk could serve as a coffee table as well as a great storage space for sweaters or towels and other linens.

5. **Once you're organized and the party is over, you'll have to work every
    day to maintain order.** Each time you remove an item from its home,
    you have to make a choice. Will you (1) put it back where it goes so you
    can find it the next time or (2) just put it down and go on a hunting
    expedition the next time you need it?

Getting organized may seem like an impossible task, but you can do it. And
unlike dieting or exercising, the results are immediate!

*Provided by Peggy Duncan, CEO of the Duncan Resource Group, Inc. Learn more about her
firm by visiting the Web at www.duncanresource.com.*

An Organized Read

If you're looking for some inspiration to get your organizing juices
flowing, you'll have plenty of options. Try to look beyond the hype
when you approach the task of organizing—just pick up a book on
the subject. So far, I have read seven books on organizing and simplifying and all of them offered some good tips. I particularly liked
Organizing from the Inside Out by Julie Morgenstern. This book not
only offers suggestions for how to get (and stay) organized, but also
helps you get to the root of your disorganization tendencies in a
chapter titled What's Holding You Back? This chapter helped me
identify my "psychological obstacles," and I was able to create a
plan to overcome them.

I also enjoyed *Simplify Your Life* by Elaine St. James. In this
book, St. James lays out one hundred steps you can take toward creating a more simple life. It was a quick, easy read, which is probably
part of what makes it so enjoyable. Rather than giving very complicated instructions or systems on how to clear out and simplify, St.
James seems to take a more inspirational approach. And if you're

interested in simplifying on a deeper level, *Inner Simplicity*, also by St. James, is a great read too.

Creating "Organization Central"

In addition to organizing your "things," it's a good idea to organize the day-to-day workings of your life. It sounds like a huge undertaking doesn't it? Well it can be, but a good way to begin is by creating a "center" in your apartment where you can go to keep up with many of the things that make your life so busy.

I like to locate this center in my kitchen, since that's where I spend a lot of time and where many family planning discussions take place. My organization center includes the following:

- **A family calendar.** It's one place where I record appointments, school meetings, birthdays, and other important dates. Make sure everyone who lives with you refers to it and records events on one central calendar to avoid confusion and missed commitments.

- **A notepad and pen.** Since I work from home, I get lots of phone calls. I place a notepad and pen right next to the phone, so when I'm not available, whoever answers has no excuse for forgetting to pass along a message!

- **A magnetic dry erase board.** I have one of these fabulous inventions attached to my refrigerator. (Mine came with magnetic strips glued onto the back.) I use it for jotting down my shopping list as I realize I need items, as well as for leaving notes to family members.

- **A bill holder.** I found a very inexpensive bill holder made of thin (but durable) cardboard. It has thirty-one numbered slots in it, which correspond to each day of the month. When I open a bill, I slip it into the number that corresponds with the bill's due date. No more guess-

ing and no more opening bills four or five times to check
the due date.

❖ **A bulletin board.** I use my bulletin board as a catch-all
for everything from party invitations to pizza coupons.
(It's also a great place to display photos and kids' artwork.) If you'd like to create an extra large bulletin board
using a door in your apartment, see the innovative
Bulletin Board Door Project in the sidebar on page 33.

❖ **A hook and folder for everyone.** Next to the door, I
placed a series of hooks for jackets and a small hanging
folder for each family member. After I sign papers for
school, for example, I place them in my daughter's
folder. On her way out, she checks her folder to see
whether there's anything in it that needs to go with her.
(It's also a great place to deposit lunch money!) I also
leave things for myself in my own folder, such as
coupons and letters I need to mail.

Before I created my family's organization center, we had some
difficulty getting the right things to the right people on the right
day. Now that we have a center that works for everyone, staying
organized is much easier than we ever dreamed it could be!

The Dreaded Clothing Closet

When you get dressed in the morning, how does the experience
unfold? Have you ever rummaged through your closet looking for
a certain belt and located every single belt you own *except* the one
you need? Have you ever stood looking in your closet thinking "I
have nothing to wear," yet you are surrounded by a more-than-
ample selection of just that—things to wear?

It's an age-old problem and one that seems difficult to fix at
times. But think of the impact a messy closet has on your life. First

thing in the morning, you are greeted by chaos rather than order. But there's hope.

Professional organizer Peggy Duncan offers the following strategy for tackling the area often most hard hit by disorganization—your closet:

- Purge first, remembering that if you didn't wear it last year, you probably won't wear it this year. Separate the things you want to keep, and bag up the things to give away and the things to throw out.

- Purchase a closet-organizing system that provides different levels of shelving, so you can arrange shelves at different heights. This can help you create instant space even in the tiniest of closets.

- Arrange your closet, keeping like things together—all your pants/skirts, jackets, and blouses/shirts should be kept separate. (Keeping like colors together is also a time saver.) If you never mix and match, hang complete outfits together.

Illustration 1-B. Bulletin Board Door Project.

- Put items you don't use often farthest away from you.

- Use shelving products that fit over doors to create more space.

- Keep two baskets on the floor of your closet, one for dry cleaning and the other for clothes that need be repaired. Don't rehang soiled clothes.

Bulletin Board Door Project

This clever decorating project—courtesy of Wallflowers' Home Decorating Projects and Ideas (www.wallflowers.net)—requires something you probably have several of in your apartment: a door! This extra large bulletin board is great for people who work at home and have lots of notes, papers, and other documents that need to be kept in plain view. It's also great for hanging posters and makes changing them a snap—and lessens the possibility of leaving unnecessary holes on apartment walls!

Project Instructions

You will need

Iron
Fabric (we used one yard of 52"-wide fabric)
Tape
Newspaper
Scissors
Yardstick
Pencil
2 Sheets of Flash N Tack (tackable wall panels 32" by 48")
Glue (we use Beacon Fabri Tac)
Staple gun with 1/4" staples
13 #6 × 1 1/4" drywall screws (see note below)
Screwdriver
Art brush
Paint for the buttons (we use Americana in Olive Green)
13 3/4" wood furniture buttons
Jigsaw or utility knife

How to do it

Note: An alternative to screwing the fabric panels in place is using self-adhering hook and loop tape attached to the door and the panels. If you chose this method, be sure to stick the tape to the fabric on the back sides of the panels. If the tape is stuck to the board, it will come off easily, pulling part of the board with it. Also use strips as long as the shape on all sides. (See example in illustration 1-B.)

1. Iron fabric if necessary.

2. Tape the newspapers together to make a pattern one inch smaller than the door on all four sides.

3. Cut a circle out of the pattern just large enough to slide over the door-knob.

4. Tape the pattern to the door so it sits one inch inside all four edges of the door.

5. Place a yardstick over the pattern so the top edge is even with the top right-hand corner and the bottom edge is at an angle to end a few inches above the doorknob. (The yardstick won't be long enough for you to draw the entire line.)

6. Trace along the top and bottom of the yardstick, then slide it to the doorknob to trace the second part of the line. By tracing along both sides of the yardstick, there will be approximately 1" between the shapes.

7. Continue tracing both sides of the yardstick to create all four sections.

8. Number the shapes 1 to 4 starting at the top and working from the right to the bottom.

9. Cut out the shapes.

10. Tape the shapes to the tack board.

    Hint: To conserve board, it may be necessary to flip over the patterns for the shapes. Use a pencil to label the back side of the pattern or on the board, to remind you to cover the back side of the tack board, not the front.

11. Cut out the tack board.

12. Lay the fabric face down.

13. Place the tack board on top of the fabric allowing a 2" gap between boards.

14. Cut the fabric around the tack board so the fabric pieces will be 1" larger on all sides than the board.

15. With fabric still centered under the board, move a single shape in front of you. Run a bead of glue approximately 3/4" in from the edge on one side. Wrap the material around to the line of glue and press firmly.

16. Staple along the glued edge of the material.

Note: The staples won't hold the fabric securely but they will hold until the glue dries.

17. Repeat along all edges, folding the corners as you work.

18. Repeat to finish all shapes.

19. Following the numbers on the pattern, arrange the shapes in position on the floor.

20. Place shape 1 in place 1" from the top edge and 1" from the left edge. Screw through the panel and into the door. Use one screw set in from each corner.

Hint: Sometimes the fabric twists, so we recommend that you turn the screw all the way in, then unscrew a few turns. With one hand holding the material straight, slowly rescrew into place.

21. Paint furniture buttons and allow to dry.

22. Glue furniture buttons in place over screw heads.

Reprinted with permission from Wallflowers.net.

Organizing Crafting Supplies

Any crafter will tell you that supplies can seem to multiply overnight. But sometimes you just have to hang on to that quarter-bottle of orange paint or a half-roll of silk ribbon for months before you find the perfect use for it. So what's a crafter with limited space to do?

If you're tired of crafting supplies lying all over your apartment, it's time to organize them. Try this: Purchase a few large, rectangular storage boxes. Group your crafts supplies into categories, such as sewing materials, paints and brushes, and so forth. Place item groupings into the storage boxes, and secure a large, self-adhesive label at the end of the box. On the label, write all the contents of the box in large, readable lettering. By labeling each box, you won't have to dig through several to find what you're looking for. The boxes can be placed on a bookshelf or stacked in a closet.

Checklists and Worksheet

Now that you have a decorating goals statement and a decorating worksheet, you're almost ready to get to work. In figure 1.8, you can record room and area measurements so you can purchase the appropriate items, especially furniture. (Wouldn't it be awful to get that perfect dining room table home and realize it doesn't fit in the room?)

Figure 1.9 can help you determine which tools you may need during the decorating process, particularly if you will be making some items or recycling secondhand items. Remember: You don't need to *purchase* all the tools you need to accomplish decorating your home. Be sure to check with family and friends, and ask whether you can borrow tools. Also check with your local hardware or home improvement store. Some stores will rent tools to you at a reasonable price.

Figure 1.8
Room and Area Measurements

Area	Width	Length	Doorway
Living Room			
Kitchen			
Dining room			
Home office			
Bedroom			
Bathroom			
Sunroom/porch			
Deck/balcony			

Figure 1.9
Decorating Tools

- ✔ Hammer
- ✔ Fabric glue
- ✔ Hot glue gun
- ✔ Notebook
- ✔ Nails, screws
- ✔ Beads
- ✔ Paint
- ✔ Measuring tape
- ✔ Screwdriver
- ✔ Tassels
- ✔ Paintbrushes & rollers
- ✔ Ruler
- ✔ Scissors
- ✔ Ribbon
- ✔ Sewing supplies
- ✔ Graph paper
- ✔ Sandpaper
- ✔ Fabric
- ✔ Pens, pencils
- ✔ Wire brush
- ✔ Cleaners
- ✔ Scraper
- ✔ Paint thinner
- ✔ Paint stripper

Creating a Decorating Notebook

I love home and garden and decorating-related magazines; I just can't get enough of them. From *Martha Stewart Living* to *Mary Engelbreit's Home Companion* to *Victoria,* I scour through a pile of publications each month and get wonderful ideas from them.

Illustration 1-C. Decorating Notebook.

But at one point a few years ago, stacks of magazines began to take over my bedroom (and living room and kitchen). In addition to taking up space, I had so many of them that locating information was nearly impossible. On the occasion that I needed to seek out a specific project or photograph, it would often take me hours to sort through my collection to find it. And sometimes, I would not find it at all.

If you're in the same position, I assure you there's hope, and you don't have to give up or even cut back on your magazine consumption. It's simply a matter of "clipping and keeping." To capture magazine photographs, articles, and other decorating information and make them accessible for later use, you can create a decorating notebook. In addition to saving samples clipped from magazines, you can also use your notebook to organize paint samples, wallpaper samples, fabric swatches, and anything else you may wish to use later.

Creating your own decorating notebook is easy (see example in illustration 1-C). Try these simple steps:

1. Purchase a notebook, such as a three-ring binder with hole-punched paper, a scrapbook, a photo album, or a

spiral-bound notebook. (I like to use photo albums, so I can move things around easily.)

2. Create "sections", either by room (living room, kitchen, etc.) or by decorating category (walls, flooring, etc.) or both.

3. When you find a photo, paint sample, or other item you'd like to save, secure it onto the appropriate page. You can also attach contractor bids, business cards, printouts from decorating sites on the Internet, and even your own sketches.

4. Once it's complete, be sure to take your decorating notebook along with you when you go shopping!

Ideas, Tips, and Tricks

If your budget isn't working out, or if you'd like to trim some areas and transfer the budget dollars into other areas or spend more on special purchases, consider these money-saving tips:

❖ When searching for secondhand sofas and chairs, look for comfort and a shape that appeals to you. If you don't like the upholstery, purchase or sew slipcovers in the fabric of your choice.

❖ Remember that coffee tables don't have to be coffee tables. Opt for an old trunk or crate, and you have not only a place to set your drink but also extra storage.

❖ If you find a piece of furniture (e.g., a table) that's affordable and well constructed but you don't care for the look, purchase it and paint it the same color as the room where it will live. Painting furniture the same color as the walls makes it less noticeable.

If you need more help in getting organized, try the following:

◉ Schedule organizing time like you would schedule an appointment. Pick a start and stop time, and pencil it in on your calendar.

◉ Buy some graph paper and sketch out all of your rooms. Draw furniture right on the paper, or make small cutouts so you can try different arrangements. (Designers do this.)

◉ When you open your mail, make sure to feed your "circular file" (a.k.a. your trash can or recycle bin) as you go through it. Opening mail next to your trash can helps you get used to pitching unwanted items immediately.

◉ If you're very serious about setting up your space perfectly and buying the right furniture for your apartment, check your local software store for home design software.

Places to Shop

You've sorted through your belongings and you've gotten everything organized. You know just what you have and what you need to purchase, to decorate your apartment exactly the way you want it. What stands between you and your dream place now? Perhaps a few items, or, maybe many items. Either way, it's time to go shopping! Today's budget decorating enthusiasts have many choices for where they locate the perfect—or not so perfect, yet recyclable—home furnishings and accessories.

Retail Stores

As much as I love flea markets and other such places, there are certain things I *always* purchase at stores. But when it comes to decorating, there are several different types of places to shop. Here's a look at a few.

Discount Stores

I admit it—I was once a decorating snob. It had nothing to do with being wealthy, because I am not and never have been. Still, years ago, when I thought of furniture and accessories, I didn't think Wal-Mart, Kmart, Target, and other such stores were the places to go for these types of items. Then along came the queen of all things domestic, Martha Stewart, and things began to change. Kmart introduced Martha's home accessories, and this fabulous line included everything from paint to linens. But as much as I love Martha's style, I wasn't going to be so easily convinced. It took me a while longer to warm up to the idea that many of my decorating dilemmas could be solved by a discount chain.

In the 1980s when I began living in my first, post–college dorm apartments, I needed to stock up on home accessories. As I prepared to move from Florida to Georgia after graduating from college, my parents rendered most of my college apartment furnishings "worthless," and they wouldn't let me take them to my new place. (I believe the word "disgraceful" was used by dear old Dad to describe my horrible, ripped sofa, as he heaved it into the apartment complex's dumpster.) After my parents declared most of my home furnishings "unusable," they gave me $1,000 and said, "Spend it wisely, because there *won't* be more where that came from."

Shortly after I arrived in my new apartment in Georgia, it was time to spruce up my place. (It sat pathetically empty for weeks, because all that I owned was a bed, a chair, a stereo, and my clothing.) So, I hit a few fancy department stores in a nearby mall. I found beautiful linens and accessories, but they were far out of my price range. A comforter for $350? Towels for $30 a piece? Yikes! I knew if I shopped at these stores for my apartment needs, my $1,000 wouldn't get me very far.

My roommate told me about some stores dedicated to home decor such as towels, linens, and shower curtains. These places seemed a bit better, but still, I could only afford the sale items. So, for a long time, I bought nothing. Then on the way home from work one day, I stopped at Wal-Mart to pick up some batteries. I decided to give their home accessories department a try—and wow, I never imagined the selection! The prices were reasonable, and I purchased most of what I needed for my new place on that one shopping trip. With the adrenaline of discount retail shopping pulsing through my veins, I hit Kmart the next day. Again, the selection was great, and the prices were unbeatable.

So what did I learn through all of this? I learned that having great decorating sense and style has little to do with how much you spend and the name of the store where you spend it. It has much more to do with having a great eye, knowing what you like, and being (even just a little) creative.

Don't forget to check your local Sunday newspaper for sale announcements. The larger discount store chains also now have Web sites that feature sophisticated, online ordering systems. This comes in very handy if you live off the beaten path, far from where these stores are physically located.

Department Stores

Okay, it's true, many department stores (especially those in malls) can have some pretty pricey home decorating departments. Still, it's a good idea to check them out anyway. You may find a style you like and be able to find a less expensive version somewhere else.

Also remember that many department stores hold white sales, and often the savings are quite substantial. And don't forget to check the clearance section while you're there!

Home Decorating Stores

You know the places—Bed, Bath & Beyond, Linens & Things, Linen Loft, and many others. Although you may find less expensive items in discount stores, home decorating stores tend to have enormous selections. So if you're looking for a comforter to match a very specific turquoise color, for instance, these types of places might be your best bet.

I also found a wonderful place recently—Ballard Designs—that is an outlet center for the company that publishes the popular decorating catalog. Although most items are higher than I tend to go, they have wonderful sales on slightly scratched or dented items that make the trip worth it.

The lesson here: Be sure to check your local telephone book for similar types of clearance centers and outlets.

Yard and Estate Sales

Ask an ardent yard sale shopper, and they'll tell you that shopping at yard sales is addictive. They're also likely to have some great stories of their yard sale excursions. In my own circle of yard-saling friends, I've heard reports of people striking up new friendships, finding priceless treasures for just a few bucks, and running into old pals they haven't seen in years, all while attending yard sales.

Are You a Yard Sale Novice or a Pro?

So you think this yard sale stuff is pretty easy, right? Well, seasoned yard sale enthusiasts will tell you it's not as easy as it looks. Getting the right bargains takes a lot of thought, planning and care, and most of all, practice.

What kind of yard sale shopper are you? See the following chart to determine your skill level:

Novice	Pro
Arrives when a yard sale is scheduled to begin	Arrives a half hour early, sits in the car sipping coffee and reviewing maps
Pays the asking price	Always asks for a 5- to 10-percent discount
Brings checks, credit cards, and a little cash	Brings checks and lots of cash, especially small bills
Squints to read a price tag, since it's early/overcast/held in a dark garage	Carries a flashlight and magnifying glass at all times
Worries about the china just purchased, because it might knock around on the drive home	Carefully wraps china in towels and blankets always stashed in the trunk of the car

Changing With the Times

Years ago, yard sales were pretty simple. If someone decided to have a sale, they'd simply create a sign and hang it at the end of their street or in front of their building. Perhaps they'd even run an advertisement in the newspaper and list some of the items up for sale. When the day arrived, the ardent yard sale shoppers would be there as soon as (or even before) the seller opened for business. It was all a very neighborly tradition.

Over the past few years, the popularity of buying (and selling) goods at yard sales has become a great American pastime, but things seem just a little different. Now, I see yard sales advertised in newspapers up to several weeks before the event. In my area, I see entire neighborhoods participating in huge, highly organized multi-family yard sales, where participants split advertising fees, adhere to some predetermined rules, and tie balloons or other identifiers to their mailboxes so shoppers know which houses have the goods to sell. I visited such a neighborhood sale recently, and I got stuck in my first ever, yard-sale-spurred traffic jam.

The Internet has also helped the yard sale evolve from its humble beginnings. Sites like Yard Sale Search (www.yardsalesearch .com) and Yard Sales USA (www.yardsales-usa.com) offer site visitors searchable databases of yard sales being held all over the country. Yard Sale Search even offers bulletin boards, a chat room, and articles for yard sale enthusiasts. Yard Sales.com (www.yardsales .com) also offers a searchable database of yard sales in the United States and can even generate a map to the sale location. And thanks to modern technology, you don't even need a yard to hold a yard sale anymore. Yard Sale.com (www.yardsale.com) is a virtual yard sale that enables sellers to post their items and sell them to site visitors using an auction-style method.

If you're new to yard sale shopping (and even if you're not), here are a few hints that may help you maximize your shopping experience:

◉ **Check the newspaper.** Many people who host yard sales place advertisements several days or even a week in advance, and checking your local newspaper is the best way to learn about those held in your area.

◉ **Plan your path.** After you've decided which sales you'd like to hit, map out your journey ahead of time. Internet-based mapping tools (e.g., Mapquest at www.mapquest .com) give you door-to-door directions, so you won't have to leave finding a sale location to chance. You can also purchase software that offers the same feature.

◉ **Don't forget other sources.** Residential neighborhoods aren't the only places that hold yard sales. Check local bulletin boards at schools, churches, recreation centers, and grocery stores for church, school, and organization sales. These sales are often much larger than single- or multifamily yard sales and also offer a wider variety of items and styles.

◉ **Take cash.** Make sure you have ample cash with you, since many sellers are reluctant to take personal checks. Bargaining also works better when the seller can see you have cash in hand as you try to finagle them down on prices.

◉ **Start out bright and early.** My yard sale sources tell me the best stuff is often "snatched up shortly after dawn." Don't risk it—get up and out as early as possible.

◉ **Don't be shy.** Get up your nerve and learn to negotiate with sellers. They *want* to sell this piece or they wouldn't be there. Negotiating tends to work best near the end of the day.

Estate Sales

Estate sales are often held when a person dies and his or her belongings need to be sold, for whatever reason. In addition, a home owner who is moving to another state, or perhaps retiring to a smaller residence, may hold an estate sale to clear out some belongings. Often, estate sales take place right in a home, so you can see how the furnishings look in a true home environment.

When I visited an estate sale recently, I was amazed at the turnout. I arrived a half-hour before the sale was scheduled to begin, and I was the thirtieth person in line. In front of me were many antique dealers and collectors, some of whom had arrived more than an hour before the sale opened.

Although I have not found the estate sales in my area to have as much reasonably priced merchandise as the yard sales, they are definitely worth a try. Check the classified section of your newspaper for announcements.

The World's Longest Yard Sale

If multifamily yard sales excite you, hold on to your hat.

Since 1987, yard sale shoppers have flocked to see an incredible site that gives testament to the popularity of yard sales in the United States—the World's Longest Outdoor Yard Sale. The extravaganza began as an effort to get travelers off the interstate highways and onto the less traveled roads through the small towns of Tennessee.

These days, the 450-mile route spans parts of Tennessee, Kentucky, and Alabama, all on Highway 127. What will you find there? Antiques, clothing, furniture—you name it, you'll probably find it. Lodging is also plentiful on the corridor, no matter what style of accommodations you prefer. From campgrounds to hotels to bed-and-breakfasts, you'll find a great place to rest your head after a fun-filled day of more bargaining opportunities than you could count.

For more information on the World's Longest Outdoor Yard Sale, check out www.127sale.com.

Flea Markets

Flea markets, swap meets, whatever you call them, every budget decorator should visit one now and then. They've been around for many years, and they're some of the best places I know of to search for inexpensive and stylish home furnishings and accessories.

"What are flea markets like?" I was once asked by a friend who had never attended one. Well, that was a difficult question to answer. As difficult, in fact, as answering the question "What is a store?" Flea markets come in a variety of sizes and styles, just as stores do. For instance, there are convenience stores, grocery stores, jewelry stores, and even roadside fruit stands. Along those same lines, flea markets can range from a few vendors laying their items on tablecloths on the ground, to a few dozen in makeshift booths, to a few hundred or a thousand housed in elaborate, indoor facilities complete with air conditioning and restaurants.

The first flea market I ever attended was a life-changing experience for me (although I didn't know it at the time). When I was young, my father often disappeared just after dawn on Saturday mornings, and I knew he was attending what he called a "swap meet." So one day I accompanied him, and I saw the vendors setting up tables on the dusty square of property that served as a drive-in movie parking lot at night. On that day, I saw things for sale like antiques, socks, clothing, and lots of vinyl records and eight-track tapes. I was seven years old, and the year was 1971. I bought a few record albums that day, and I was thrilled with my accomplishment of bargaining the salesman down $0.50 on my purchase. I became a frequent swap meet shopper after that.

Recently, my father came to visit, and we attended another flea market. This one was far from the first one we'd visited and different in most every way. I dragged my father out of bed early and rushed him through breakfast. I told him if we didn't get there before 9 A.M., there would be no parking near the entrance and we'd have a long walk. We rushed off and made the thirty-minute drive, and I dictated to him a list of items I was hoping to find, as I drove. We walked in the front gate and had our pick of hundreds of booths, some housed inside buildings complete with bathrooms and food vendors. We spent about three hours inspecting and purchasing antiques and secondhand items. We stayed until we'd purchased so many things, we could not carry anything else—and that was our cue that it was time to go home. I was as pleased with my purchases on that recent trip as I was in 1971. Except now I'm thirty-six, and my father is in his seventies. But the feeling is always the same—the excitement of a bargain found and a day well spent.

So, have you been bitten by the bug yet? If you have, you may be nodding your head saying, "Yep, it's exciting alright." If not, I encourage you to give it a shot. And to help make your flea market experience productive, I offer the following suggestions:

- ❖ **Take your list and try to stick to it.** I keep a running list of everything I need (and want) handy at all times, in my purse. At flea markets, the list helps me stay on target with my purchases.

- ❖ **Get comfy.** Wear the comfiest shoes and clothes you have, because it might be a very long, tiring day. And be sure to wear clothes you don't mind getting dirty.

- ❖ **Invest in a wheeled cart.** You can get inexpensive, fold-up carts (the kind you use to carry your luggage from your car into the airport) at most discount stores. Take this wise investment along and you won't have to make the long trek back to your car on days when you find lots of treasures. Another tip—secure an empty crate onto the cart to hold smaller items efficiently.

Ten Reasons to Shop at Flea Markets

If you've never visited a flea market, you just don't know what you've been missing! In addition to the obvious benefit of being able to pick up great things for little cash, there are even more reasons to shop at your local flea market. For instance:

1. You can locate hard-to-find items that are no longer manufactured, such as china in discontinued patterns.

2. They're open on weekends, when you may have more free time to browse at a leisurely pace.

3. You can meet lots of interesting people.

4. Unlike at most retail stores, the prices you'll find at flea markets can often be negotiated.

5. You can help the environment and conserve resources by purchasing previously owned goods.

6. You'll be able to browse a wide variety of goods at a single location.

7. You can get to know flea market vendors who can keep an eye out for items you're trying to locate.

8. You won't need to worry about experimenting if you pick up items for just a few bucks.

9. You can find out for yourself how thrilling it is to hunt for the perfect decorative treasure and find it in the most unlikely places!

10. And last but not least—shopping at flea markets is just plain fun!

❖ **Picture this; measure it out.** If you have a serious decorating challenge—such as a problem corner or a room that needs lots of help—take photographs of the room (the corner, etc.), and take the photos with you when you go shopping. Also attach a note to the photo that provides the dimensions of the area you're trying to decorate.

The Art of Garbage

If you see interior designer Carol A. Tanzi, A.S.I.D, digging in someone's trash, don't worry. She hasn't fallen on hard times. In fact, times are quite good for this Burlingame, California–based designer, and garbage is part of the reason.

It all began in the 1960s, when Tanzi worked at Macy's department store. She found some Styrofoam and Plexiglas and created an artistic display from the materials by placing white geometric shapes on the Plexiglas. The response: "People just flipped out," she said.

A few decades later, Tanzi was working on her own as a designer, and she became the Goddess of Garbage—partly due to a tendency since childhood to makes things with junk, and largely due to her concern for the environment and wanting to reuse existing materials as much as possible.

Tanzi (who also works with new materials, depending on her clients' desires) is often amazed at the wonderful things she finds in dumpsters and garbage cans. One of her favorite finds was "a beautiful framed oil painting of Abraham Lincoln. It was leaning up again the inside wall of a dumpster." She snatched it up and gave it to a friend who collects Lincoln memorabilia. Tanzi has also created desks from discarded lumber and radiators, bookcases from discarded metal, and wall accessories and wine racks from one of her favorite materials: Styrofoam.

You may be wondering, as I was, can anyone do this, and, more important, is retrieving items from someone's garbage legal?

"Before you do it, you need to check with the rules and regulations of the city. In some cities it's legal; in some it's not," Tanzi said.

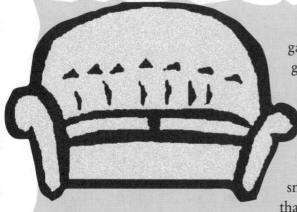

If you want something from someone's garbage and if your city or county allows garbage picking, you should always ask before you take, whether it's a business or a residence that's throwing away the item.

"If I see something I like, I try to find out who it belongs to. I go and ring the doorbell and ask if I can have it. It's smart business, and it lends the courtesy to that person," she says. The answer is almost always yes, Tanzi reports, and most people are fascinated and want to know what she has planned for their discarded items.

If you'd like to take garbage (your own or someone else's) and create some sort of home furnishings or accessories, Tanzi has the following suggestions:

- **Go for discard sofas or chairs.** If they're stained, you can use a slipcover. But be sure to clean it thoroughly before you use it.

- **Ask your friends.** It takes less courage to ask a friend whether they have anything they're ready to get rid of, than to ask a stranger.

- **Look for table bases.** Seek out pieces of wood, plaster of paris—anything interesting that can hold a surface can become a table base.

- **Ask businesses.** "Always ask at mirror and glass places if they have anything they want to give away," Tanzi says. The answer will often be yes.

- **Take a workshop.** Tanzi offers workshops frequently in the San Francisco area and travels to other parts of the country presenting them as well. Check her Web site (address below) for more information.

Learn more about Carol A. Tanzi, A.S.I.D., on her Web site: www.goddessofgarbage.com.

Antique Stores

When you think of an antique store, what do you think of? Ten years ago, my answer would have been very different than it would be today. Back then, antiques were things that were in my mother's home, not mine. Antiques were dark, heavy, and ornate, and, of course, they were quite expensive. When I thought of buying furniture, I really never thought of buying antiques. Antiques were simply too intimidating for me.

One of the first antique stores I visited alone was in Charleston, South Carolina. The place was full of $50 teacups, $3,000 sofas, and $300 first-edition books. The woman who greeted me at the door was about sixty years old, and her face and hair looked as though they had been perfectly chiseled into place. She wore a wool suit, stockings, and pumps and spoke to me in a high-brow accent, as opera music played softly in the background. My immediate urge was to run out of the store yelling "Sorry, I made a big mistake!" but I resisted. I walked around for a few minutes, afraid to touch anything, feeling ridiculously out of place in my jeans and sneakers. So went my first antique shop experience, and it helped verify my suspicion that antiques weren't quite right for me.

Then, I met Abe. Well, I don't really know Abe personally. Actually I am not really sure he exists, but I like to think he does. That's because an antique mall named Abe's is the place where my love affair with antiques began, years after my intimidating experience in the Charleston shop. I walked into Abe's for the first time several years ago, when I took a wrong turn on my way to Target. I was greeted by jeans-clad, thirty-something sale reps, cheerful big band music, and booths full of reasonably priced items. I wanted to take home everything; I wanted to make my rooms look like the booths in Abe's Antique Mall.

Since finding Abe's, I've been in hundreds of antique stores. Some are much like my original antique store experience—full of expensive china and furniture. (I rarely spend more than a few minutes in these types of places.) I have also found many stores that cater to people like me—people who love antiques but must find a bargain. If you love old stuff, you can find those kinds of places, too, and you can make great use of the stuff you find there. It just takes a little practice.

But how do you practice? It's easy, once you get the hang of it. Just find some inexpensive items in an antique store and think about them carefully. Briefly consider the traditional use for each piece. For instance, if you see a wood mantel, you might briefly tell yourself, "Yes, this is a wood mantel that goes around a fireplace." Now, take another look. Think about the possibilities for use *beyond* what you've been programmed to think. Turn it sideways, upside down, backward, and see if you get a flash of inspiration. Now you might say, "Well, it has a nice shelf on top, and it has a great, square shape. I know—I could use it as a headboard!" Bingo! You've just given an old mantel a new life.

Need some more ideas to get you going? Consider these items, all of which I've purchased recently in antique, junk, and rummage stores throughout the Southeastern United States:

* A set of small foot lockers, perfect as a storage unit for my crafts supplies. Total cost: $48

* A large, green potting table, intended for garden use but recycled into a home office desk by adding a $15 keyboard drawer for better ergonomics. Total cost: $70

* An old window, which became a coat rack when I attached three, 50-cent hooks to it. Total cost: $4.50

* A 1950s tablecloth, which was folded over a drapery bar and became a window treatment without a single stitch of thread. Total cost: $12

❖ A painted step ladder that became a perfect bedroom night table (see example in illustration 2-A), capable of holding a lamp, books, and a plant, in distinctive country style. Total cost: $13

One more lesson I learned over the years is one I repeat to people often, especially those just starting out in antique shopping and collecting. I encourage newcomers to develop as many contacts as they can and to keep in touch with them. For me, it may go something like this: When I visit an antiques store, I may see a collection of sap buckets that catch my eye. When I'm paying (or just ready to leave without a purchase), I might stop and tell

Illustration 2-A. A step ladder used as a night table.

the clerk I really love the sap buckets, that I collect garden-style antiques, and that I am always looking for them. "Oh, really?" he might reply. "Well, I got those from my brother-in-law, who has a shop across town, and he has lots of garden antiques. Anything in particular that you're looking for?" And so the conversation continues, he might call his brother-in-law, and that very afternoon I might just locate the small iron gate section I've been seeking for the past year to use as a photo holder.

Sometimes the results aren't so immediate, but developing contacts is still worthwhile. I once had a casual acquaintance I'd known for a few years. I knew what she did for a living, but never realized that she had a job on the side—as a buyer for an antiques shop. She traveled regularly to Europe and would bring back wonderful finds for the shop to sell. I mentioned to her that I love old botanical prints, especially rose prints. Months later, she called to let me know she had several rose prints in perfect condition and had acquired them on a trip overseas because she thought I might like them. She then sold them to me for 50 percent off the price they would have been if they'd ever made it into the store.

Trading, Borrowing, and Inheriting Furniture

Does all the furniture in your house need to really be yours? No, of course not! Just as you might let your friends or family members borrow other items, borrowing furniture can be just as easy. And it's often a very smart solution to a problem. Consider this scenario:

THE PROBLEM: An eighteen-year-old inherits an antique desk from a relative. But she's away at college, and her living quarters are very cramped. Plus, she's worried friends and roommates may damage it by placing drinks on top or other such things.

THE SOLUTION: Her older sister who lives in a roomy condominium offers to take good care of the piece for her, until she's ready to take it back.

THE RESULT: The younger sister doesn't have to worry about the desk fitting into her dorm room or getting damaged. The older sister is able to use the beautiful piece for four years.

Trading is another great way to fill your apartment with just the right pieces. Let's say you have a four-poster bed. But when you move to an new place, the bed just doesn't work well. Perhaps the ceilings are low and the posters are too close to a ceiling fan. But what about that friend of yours who's always admired this bed? Doesn't she have that wonderful mahogany sleigh bed you always thought was really great? The answer is simple: Propose a trade.

Before you borrow or trade furniture though, you may want to consider a few potential pitfalls:

- If you change your mind, you may politely ask for your item back, because your friend might have experienced a change of heart, too. But if your friend doesn't want to, the relationship could suffer.

- If you're trading for purposes of a better fit for a piece of furniture, measure your space and each piece *before* you trade.

- If you're borrowing or the trade is temporary, try to set a time limit on it. For instance, you could borrow for two years or until the original owner moves to a new place where it fits, whenever that may be.

When it comes to inheriting furniture, you get something for free with an added bonus: it probably comes with memories. If you inherit art or antiques, it may be a good idea to have them appraised when you receive them, especially if you have no idea of the value. This can help you determine how to care for the items properly. For instance, if a piece of furniture is valuable in its current state, you know that painting it bright purple (even if it would match your bedroom furniture) is *not* a great idea.

If you have a good relationship with a family member and feel you can do it tactfully, you can mention how much you love a piece and that you'd love to have it someday. Remember to carefully consider the other person's feelings before attempting this, and choose your words carefully.

Hot Trend: Garden-Style Decorating

Maybe you've noticed it too. Garden-style decorating has become so popular, it's difficult to miss. Cover after cover of decorating magazines show exciting ways to use garden-style furnishings and accessories in your living space. And several books have been published recently, devoted entirely to this subject.

I first noticed the trend last year as I was strolling through a large antiques market. First I came upon a booth that housed more than a thousand sap buckets, and the crowd of shoppers was so large there I had to return twice just to see the merchandise. As I continued through the market, I found booth after booth filled with garden treasures. I saw wrought iron patio furniture, picket fencing, topiaries, clay pots, garden urns, iron gates, and every garden ornament I could think of up for grabs. There is no denying it—the garden trend has arrived in a very big way.

One of the things I love most about garden-style decorating is that you can introduce it into your home environment easily and inexpensively. Here are a few ideas to get you started:

* Find a fan-shaped trellis (new or used) and lean it against a wall in your kitchen. Hang your dishtowels and pot holders on it, and it's not only beautiful but also useful.

* Turn a large clay pot into a table by placing a piece of glass or wood as a table surface. (A birdbath makes a great table base, too.)

* Use a metal watering can to display fresh flowers or a dried or silk arrangement.

* Use inexpensive picket fencing as a headboard and footboard, or take a small section of fence, glue on binder clips (found at an office supply store), and use it to hold notes, photos, and postcards.

* Trim down a fallen branch to make a one-of-a-kind curtain rod.

* Hang a window box on the inside of your window and fill it with potted flowers or plants. It's also a great place for a small, fragrant, and edible herb garden.

- Bring metal, wrought iron, and Adirondack chairs inside. Soften them up with throw pillows and quilts.

- Give an old iron gate or fence section a new life as a headboard or fireplace screen, or hang it on a wall to hold photos or bills.

- And, of course, fill your space with plants, flowers (potted and cut), topiaries, and other living garden delights.

Internet and Catalog Shopping

The Internet has touched many facets of our lives; why not turn to it for home decorating? One of the things I like best about online shopping is that often you are treated to information you might not learn otherwise (e.g., the assembly tips on IKEA's Web site—www.ikea.com).

Recently I've visited Bed, Bath & Beyond (www.bedbathandbeyond.com), Waverly (www.waverly.com), The Company Store (www.thecompanystore.com), Ballard Designs (www.ballarddesigns.com), and The Container Store (www.containerstore.com) without leaving my home! Their sites are friendly, easy to use, and look great. While you may not feel comfortable ordering entire rooms of furniture via the Web, decorative items and things like linens can be a pretty safe bet.

The wonderful thing about the Web is that you can visit stores that have no retail shop in your area. Plus, how else can I shop for a new computer workstation at 1 A.M. because I can't sleep? The retail stores in my town are closed—but the IKEA site is open for business!

Ideas, Tips, and Tricks

❖ If you have a spouse or partner that you live with and you're purchasing furniture you'll both use, try to take them along with you shop, or at least have them try out a new couch or bed before you bring it home.

❖ Clean thoroughly anything you purchase secondhand before you use it. (Be especially careful with antiques.)

❖ If you have purchased an item that has peeling paint and you like the look, add a layer of polyurethane to help halt the peeling but keep the look intact.

❖ When you're on a store's Web site, be sure to check out the sales—some specials are Internet-only.

❖ If you like a store's site, sign up for their mailing list or newsletter and you'll be notified via e-mail of sales and specials.

chapter 3

Flooring and Floor Coverings

It's something you'll find in every room in your apartment. It may be soft, hard, or somewhere in between. You walk on it; play on it; spill things on it; scrub it; vacuum it; and, if you don't like the one you've got, even curse it now and then. It provides you with color and sometimes texture, and it's the foundation for all your decorating endeavors.

It's your floor, and for better or worse, everyone's got to have one. And even if you can't make permanent changes to the flooring in your apartment such as painting or replacing it all together, there are many ways to make yours more beautiful.

Hard Flooring

Hard flooring may be made from a number of materials. Here's a look at some of the popular types of hard flooring used today:

WOOD—Consider yourself fortunate if you land an apartment with wood floors that have been well preserved. (Many apartment dwellers would love to be in your shoes!) Wood flooring is beautiful and versatile, as far as complementing different decorating styles. Think of it—wouldn't a sleek wood floor look just as grand with a Country-style decor as it would with Contemporary furnishings? Wood flooring comes in a variety of colors (or stains), and planks come in a variety of widths. Parquet wood flooring has an added bonus—it adds texture as well as the beauty of wood to a room.

VINYL—Vinyl is a durable type of flooring and can be inexpensive, depending on the quality. It is available in a large variety of colors, designs, and textures today, and this type of flooring is a very popular choice for apartment kitchens and bathrooms.

Clean Floors—the Natural Way

I never seemed to get the knack of getting my kitchen and bathroom floors really clean. I bought all the best commercial products and fancy mops. I mopped often and still, my vinyl always seemed sticky and my wood always felt oily. Then, a friend who happens to be a maid filled me in on a little secret: It was the cleaners that were making my floors sticky and oily. "Oh, great, so what I do I do now?" I asked. Her advice was so simple it seemed that it couldn't possibly be true. But it was, and here it is:

◉ Clean wood floors with a mixture of vinegar and water, heavier on the water. Add a drop or two of essential oil for an aromatic bonus. Amet's Essentials (www.ametsessentials.com), an Internet-based company, has a great selection and reasonable prices. (They also offer a catalog—see the Resources in the back of this book for details.) You can also find essential oils at some herb shops. And if you want to read up on oils and their qualities, stop by AromaWeb (www.aromaweb.com).

◉ Clean vinyl and tile floors with water and a little squirt of soap. Dr. Bronner's liquid soap works well, but a dishwashing liquid will do fine too. You can also add a bit of essential oil and vinegar if you'd like.

I began following her advice and was amazed. The sticky film that covered my kitchen floor is now a distant memory, and I no longer slip on my hardwood floors because of the oily residue. The result was simple: natural was not only cheaper and easier, but it worked better.

One word of warning if you have an apartment with lower-quality vinyl: Be careful with high-heeled shoes. I once lived in a place with vinyl flooring, and my affinity for high heels left its mark all over the kitchen floor, in the form of little cuts and dents. (Higher-quality vinyl resists better.)

LAMINATES—Laminates can be made from a variety of materials such as wood, synthetic, and plastic, and they've gotten amazingly sophisticated. A few years ago, I didn't know of anyone who would believe that a laminate created to look like a wood floor could ever pass for the real thing. Now, it's very common for anyone to mistake a laminate for real wood.

OTHER MATERIALS—You may also have hard flooring made of cement, brick, tile, terrazzo, or stone. Like the others mentioned, all of these types of hard flooring can look great if they're in good condition, and they can work nicely with various decorating styles.

Painting Your Floors

Let's say you're stuck with flooring that's in terrible shape (or one that's just really, really unattractive), and your landlord isn't willing, for whatever reason, to replace or make any significant improvements to it. You could request permission to paint the flooring. If your request is approved, you're in a great position to transform your space with a little paint and a little sweat. (Perhaps more than a little sweat, depending on the size of the area and the method you choose.)

Painting Wood

It takes a lot of courage to paint a wood floor, because once you've done it, undoing it can be *a lot* of work. (Depending on your willingness and skill level, you may even need to hire a professional if you want to return it to its original state at some point.) But if your wood floors are in terrible shape, or if they've been painted in a shade you just can't live with, painting might be a good option for you, if your landlord permits it. Go about it like this:

1. Measure the areas you wish to paint.

2. Take your measurements to a paint or home improvement store, and the staff will determine the number of gallons you need to purchase. (Be sure to only buy paint specifically made for wood flooring, and follow the directions on the can carefully.)

3. Brush on several coats, until you feel you've have achieved ample coverage.

4. Finish with several coats of polyurethane varnish.

Painting Linoleum

Normally, I'm not a skeptic—I just never believed it could be done. I would read articles and watch decorating television shows where people actually painted linoleum floors, but I remained unconvinced. Then I tried it. Okay, so I was wrong.
The truth is you can paint linoleum, and it's not even difficult. Just do the following:

1. Clean the area thoroughly—sweep and mop to remove *all* dirt and debris. Let the floor dry completely.

2. Using an acrylic-based paint, brush or roll several coats onto the floor. Allow this to dry completely (this may take up to forty-eight hours)

3. Top it off with several coats of polyurethane.

Carpeting and Rugs

Wall-to-wall carpeting is an extremely common floor covering in many apartments across the country. If your apartment has carpeting that's in decent shape and is a neutral color, it should be easy for you to work with it. Unfortunately, the carpeting in quite a few apartments doesn't seem to fall into this category. If many residents have lived in the space since the carpeting was laid, it's more likely to be in less-than-perfect shape. You may find yourself with one or more of the following problems:

❖ A color that clashes with your furnishings
❖ Areas that are faded because spills have been overcleaned by harsh cleansers
❖ Stains that just won't go away

Some apartment complexes steam-clean or shampoo carpeting just before a new renter moves in or require the exiting renter to do this. Still, I've moved into several apartments where the carpeting was sporting damage beyond anything a mere steam cleaning could rectify. So I simply found creative ways to live with it or work around it.

Using Rugs to Change Your Floorscape

If you have carpeting (or even hard flooring) you just don't like, and you're unable to make permanent changes because it's against the rules, what can you do? Do what you'd do for anything else you want to hide—dress it up!

Area rugs are an attractive and functional way to disguise (or even just enhance) your existing flooring, add color and texture, and define an area. For instance, you may have a floor plan that offers a combined living room and dining room. Placing one area rug in the living room (with furniture positioned along the sides and a coffee table near the center) and one in the dining room (centered under the table) can visually separate one large space into two functional areas.

Rugs can also help you create less structured areas. For instance, a rug with two chairs and a table at the edges creates a "conversation nook," and a rug with a desk creates a home office area.

The Many Faces of Area Rugs

Ethnic-style rugs (see example in illustration 3-A) are great for introducing certain colors, textures, and moods into a room. The more interesting ones are great conversation pieces and can even become the focal point for a room. I know designers and design-conscious people who often select a rug first, use it as an inspiration piece, and literally build the rest of the room around the colors and design found in the rug.

Ethnic rugs can also help introduce a specific style into a room or even a whole apartment. For instance, you may want to decorate your living room in a Native American style. If you don't have many furnishings in the style and can't purchase much at once, a large Navajo rug in the room's center helps you make big strides in that direction. You can then add accessories as you go, to complement the look even further. Oriental and kilim rugs, also quite popular now, are widely available at a various prices.

Illustration 3-A. Ethnic rugs.

Jute and sisal rugs have become extremely popular over the past few years. You can find them everywhere from Pottery Barn to the local flea market. They have interesting texture and are often very affordable. Jute and sisal look great in casual settings, come in a vari-

Your Nose Knows

How do you know if an apartment is clean before you have time to look around and inspect for visual evidence? Right—the smell! I must admit I'm a fragrance junkie, and keeping my place smelling good is almost as important to me as having it look good.

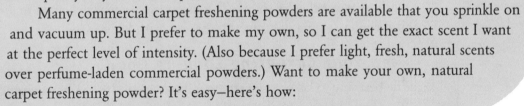

Flowers and potpourri are good ways to inject a pleasant scent into specific rooms, but when your carpeting smells clean and fresh, it can really improve the air quality of your entire apartment.

Many commercial carpet freshening powders are available that you sprinkle on and vacuum up. But I prefer to make my own, so I can get the exact scent I want at the perfect level of intensity. (Also because I prefer light, fresh, natural scents over perfume-laden commercial powders.) Want to make your own, natural carpet freshening powder? It's easy—here's how:

1. Start with a box of plain baking soda. (It's inexpensive, so purchase large boxes if you can find them. You'll save even more in the long run.)

2. Separate out enough to sprinkle in each room, and place it in a container.

3. Add a few drops of essential oil (available at health food stores, herb shops, and on the Web—see the Resources in the back of this book). Secure a lid onto the container and shake it up vigorously.

4. Sprinkle lightly on your carpeting, let it sit for a few minutes, then vacuum it up.

ety of colors and patterns, and can also be painted. The drawback is this: If you really want something soft and cushy beneath your toes, you'll probably be disappointed. Also, all those cracks and crevices can trap dirt and make these rugs difficult to keep clean.

Wool rugs tend to be more expensive, but they are extremely durable. If you're looking for a floor covering investment that will last many years, they're a good choice. *Acrylic, nylon, and polyester rugs* are worthy alternatives if you like the look and feel of wool but can't afford the real thing. They also clean up well and tend to last.

Cotton rugs are my current favorite. I find them at discount stores at affordable prices. They are often very soft and come in a variety of colors and designs. Although they are not the most durable type of area rugs, you can throw them into the washing machine when they're soiled. This easy cleanup makes them a practical choice for many budget decorators with busy lives.

Keep Your Carpeting Looking Good

The best way to keep your carpeting looking good is to keep it clean. It's a good idea to invest in a vacuum cleaner, although it need not be an expensive one. Also try to follow these carpet care suggestions:

- Vacuum well-traveled areas once or twice a week—more often if you have a pet that sheds hair.

- Keep a supply of vacuum bags on hand, so you're not caught empty-handed when your bag is full and you have friends arriving for a dinner party in ten minutes.

- Keep your carpeting (and your entire apartment) smelling fresh by creating your own carpet freshening powder (see "Your Nose Knows" sidebar on page 67).

- Take care of spills immediately so they don't leave a lasting impression (see "Keep It Clean, Folks" sidebar on page 69).

Keep It Clean, Folks

It's bound to happen—and often. Typically, it will occur just after you've vacuumed, or maybe even steam-cleaned or shampooed your carpeting. Whether you have kids who tip a cup of juice or friends who trip with soda in hand, the dreaded spill is an unavoidable fact of life.

But fear not—cleaning up a spill isn't as futile as it seems, if you do it right. Just follow these stain removal instructions from a Georgia-based carpet manufacturer:

1. Treatment of the affected area should begin immediately upon discovery. The more time that elapses before treatment, the more difficult a stain will be to remove.

2. First scrape food spills gently with a spoon or dull knife, removing as much as possible.

3. Always work from the outer edge of the stain toward the center to avoid spreading. Blot; do not rub or scrub, as the carpet may fuzz.

4. When using a mild detergent, use a clear, nonbleach laundry detergent. Do not use cloudy detergents as they can leave a sticky residue. Use only 1/4 teaspoon of detergent to thirty ounces of water. Follow detergent cleaning with clear water rinsing and then blot to dry as much as possible.

Stain removal information courtesy of Mohawk Industries, Dalton, Georgia. Information reprinted with permission. Visit Mohawk on the Web at www.mohawkcarpet.com.

Creating Your Own Floor Cloth

I'd never heard of a floor cloth until a few years ago. Now they're everywhere, and some are so beautiful they truly look like pieces of art. At a folk art show in Atlanta a few months ago, I saw a collection of floor cloths that were truly stunning, like fine art. They were so beautiful, in fact, that the artist who created them had arranged them on the floor of her booth and people were going out of their way to step over them instead of on them. People were afraid to walk on them, she told me, as she encouraged me to step right on them.

What's that, you say—you're not an artist so you can't create beautiful floor cloths? Sure you can! You don't have to be an artist to create a floor cloth. Just follow these simple instructions.

Materials

Medium-weight artist's canvas (from an art supply or fabric store)
Latex paint
Acrylic paints, paint markers, brushes
Polyurethane or varnish (4–6 coats)
Liquid rubber backing (if desired)

Steps

1. Lay canvas on a large flat surface and secure.
2. Cover the surface with a base color using latex paint.
3. Begin painting freehand or with stencils until you have achieved your desired design.
4. Allow paint to dry completely.
5. Cover with several coats of polyurethane.
6. If desired, apply liquid rubber to the back, to make the floor cloth more slip-resistant.
7. To clean, simply mop with soapy water.

Ideas, Tips, and Tricks

❖ Want to add some unexpected interest to a room? Try using two area rugs (small to medium-size) and placing them at interesting angles, with at least one corner of one rug overlapping part of the other.

❖ To paint a sisal rug:

1. Buy a stencil (or create your own from self-adhesive paper).

2. Tape the stencil onto rug, and cover other areas.

3. Spray light coats of paint onto the stencil (keep your area well ventilated).

4. Remove stencil and continue until the design has been applied to all the desired areas.

❖ You know those dents furniture can leave in your carpeting, when furniture's been in the same place for a while? Fill them back out by gently raking a fork across the affected area.

❖ Dress up a cement floor (such as on a patio or porch) by transforming it into a faux brick or terra cotta tile floor. For brick, purchase an inexpensive brick-pattern stencil and paint. For tile, paint the entire floor gray, then create a large "tile stamp" (just a square with not-so-straight sides) out of foam or a sponge. Apply your tile paint color to the foam stamp and apply to the floor, one at a time.

Walls

once heard a famous author interviewed, describing how she had decorated her home office. She told her interviewer she keeps absolutely nothing on the wall facing her writing desk—it's just bare and white. She keeps it this way, she said, so she can catch the ideas as they appear to her, without any distractions.

I thought it was an interesting concept, keeping a wall completely unadorned to help her visualize what her inner voice of creativity was trying to tell her. It inspired me to take a careful look at my own home office and ponder why I'd decorated it in a particular way. From my chair I can see many things on my walls, including a Mexican folk art cross covered in Milagros charms, a mirror with a sun-shaped frame, an antique plate and teacup collection, and an old gilded picture frame with no art inside it. For me, being surrounded by these things (and the memories they carry) is what inspires me and makes me happy and secure while I work.

So, what kinds of walls make you happy? Do you like the sleek, unobtrusive look of mostly blank walls? Would you prefer to be surrounded by colorful art in every room?

Or is your idea of a perfectly decorated wall one that is covered with framed photographs of your family, friends, and perhaps favorite places?

Before you break out the hammer and nails and start hanging anything, sit back and think carefully for a moment. How you decorate your walls should be dictated by how you like to live and how you want your apartment to make you (and those who visit you) feel. Remember that decorating goals statement you labored over in chapter 1? Well, it's time to get it out again. Review it carefully, and map out what you'll display on your apartment walls. Remember—you have no one to please but yourself.

Paint and Wallpaper

Painting apartment walls can be precarious business, particularly if your place is a rental. Some landlords do not permit painting of any kind. Others have no such restriction, and residents are free to paint, although they may be required to follow some established rules. In still other apartments, residents are permitted to paint, but walls must be repainted a certain color (often white) when they move out.

Before you paint (or wallpaper) any of your walls, check with your landlord. Even if your lease prohibits it, check anyway; rules change from time to time, and your original agreement may not reflect the most current rules. Also, if you live in a rental apartment that desperately needs to be painted and you want to tackle the task, try to negotiate it. Your landlord may let you do it, just to save the expense and effort. However, always be sure to ask about color and other restrictions, such as rules on the use of textured paints.

Coloring Your World

Let's say you live in a rental that allows painting, or you own your apartment or condo, so you can do as you please. Lucky you! Painting is one of the easiest, most inexpensive ways to transform your living space.

Consider the following, as you prepare to paint:

❖ Choose colors that go well with your current furniture and accessories, unless you plan to buy new stuff. Resist the urge to buy a color just because it's the latest trend, particularly if it's an uncommon color. Accessories to match might be hard to find once the trend has faded.

❖ If you must repaint your walls white or another light color before you move out, think twice before choosing dark colors for your space. Painting over a dark color with a light color will require several coats, adding up to greater expense and effort at move-out time.

❖ If possible, paint before you move in all your belongings. Placing dropcloths on an empty floor is much easier than moving furniture to the center of the room and covering it, as well as your flooring or carpeting.

❖ Tape off trimwork, or use a shielding tool when painting for a neat and clean look.

❖ Have all the appropriate tools on hand before you begin: brushes, rollers, tape, edgers, a ladder, and dropcloths. (And don't buy all of these items—check with friends and family first, who may be happy to lend you some or all of them.)

❖ Measure the areas you will be painting before you go out to buy paint. Take the measurements to the paint store clerk, who'll be able to calculate exactly how much paint you need.

Paint Finishing Techniques

If you're going to paint, why not consider trying a fun, creative technique, instead of just painting on one flat, ordinary color? Most of these techniques incur minimal (or no) extra expense, although most require additional time and effort. But remember: you won't be painting often. Spending more time on this task and doing a good job the first time is definitely worth the effort. And you'll confirm this each time you sit in a beautifully painted room in your home!

Here are some of today's most popular techniques:

- **Sponging.** Apply a base color directly onto the wall using a sea sponge. Mix the second (latex paint with glaze) and sponge it on as well. This treatment adds depth and the illusion of texture to any room.

- **Combing.** Apply paint to the area. While the paint is still wet, drag a comb (specially for painting) across a section to make "stripes." This technique works well if you apply a base coat, let it dry, apply a second coat, then comb through it while it's still wet.

- **Ragging.** Apply color (a latex paint and glaze mixture) to the wall using a rag. Randomly rotate and roll the rag as you apply paint. Blot the excess paint as you go to avoid drips.

- **Stenciling.** Hold (or lightly tape) the stencil onto the section of wall you wish to decorate. Apply paint onto the stencil lightly with a stenciling brush or sponge. (Tip: When stenciling, use very little paint on your brush or sponge. This will help stop paint from seeping under the stencil and beyond the outline of the design.)

You can purchase stencils at home improvement stores, design stores, paint stores, and crafts stores. Many designs, especially the simpler ones, can be purchased for just a few dollars. You can also order very artistic, elaborate stencils (also more expensive, though) from companies such as Dressler Stencil Company, American Home Stencils, and The Stencil Shoppe. (See the Resources in the back of this book for contact information.) These and other specialty stencil companies offer many related designs that, when used together, make it fairly easy for a novice to paint an entire wall mural, such as an elaborate outdoor garden scene complete with a fountain and benches.

Wallpapering Your Walls

Wallpapering entire rooms is typically more expensive than painting. (Unless, of course, you find a super clearance sale or pick up rolls at a yard sale!) Many renters do not feel that wallpapering is worth the effort and cost, unless they plan to stay put for a long time (and the landlord permits it) or they own the place.

But don't give up on the idea of wallpapering just yet. Traditionally, when people think of wallpaper, they think of entire rooms covered with it, particularly rooms like kitchens and bathrooms. But using wallpaper can be less costly and very effective if you use it *in moderation*. For instance:

* Use a patterned wallpaper on just one "accent wall" to add interest, color, and texture to a room.
* Add a wallpaper border at the ceiling line or at chair-rail level (whether or not you have an actual chair rail) for a great effect.
* Add wallpaper in your kitchen as a backsplash between your cabinets and your countertops.

If you decide to use wallpaper, the available selections may seem almost limitless. In fact, a trip to a wallpaper store can be a little overwhelming for many people—especially when you see mile-high bookshelves overflowing with pattern books. So, just take a deep breath and remain calm. When you hit stores in search of the perfect wallpaper, remember these tips:

- ๑ Bring home the biggest sample the store will allow.

- ๑ Hold the wallpaper sample against your furniture and accessories and see how they look together. Examine it in dim light, in bright light, and in sunlight. Know that swatch intimately before you decide to buy!

- ๑ Consider the pattern—large patterns do not repeat as often as smaller patterns, so they are harder to line up, and the waste (therefore, the cost) is greater.

Removable Wallpaper

It was bound to happen sooner or later. Someone has gone and invented a wallpaper (or wallpaper-like items) that you can put up and pull down in a snap. Several types of removable wallpaper and wall decorations are available today:

- ❖ **Cling-ons or removable decals.** Okay, they're not exactly wallpaper. I saw these for the first time ten years ago, when some apartment-dwelling friends had a baby and wanted to decorate a nursery but had a "no painting or wallpapering" rule in their complex. They purchased a cling-on train set, and the result was adorable and conveniently temporary!

- ❖ **Removable border and cutouts.** They can go on walls, furniture, cabinets, or any surface you'd like. Wallies Wallpaper Cutouts (www.wallies.com) has a great selection, and you can order right from their Web site. You can also find other brands of removable wallpaper at decorating stores.

What Your Hue Says About You

Have you ever visited a home improvement warehouse store and stood before one of the large paint selection displays that holds hundreds of samples? Talk about feeling overwhelmed! Unless you have a specific color in mind, paint shopping can be complicated business.

A good way to begin narrowing the field of color choices is by determining the mood you're trying to create and then selecting a color accordingly. Decide which of the phrases sounds most like you, and see what colors might help you achieve it.

* *Brrrrr—I want to warm this place up!* For a warm effect, go for yellows, browns, and ambers.
* *Let's have a party!* To crank up your decorating volume, choose intense colors like bright red or vivid orange.
* *I'm a minimalist, and I like things clean and simple.* Stick with whites, grays, and beiges, and you'll always be happy.
* *Stay calm, everyone.* Try pastel greens, blues, and pinks to create a tranquil retreat.

Once you find the colors you like, you may be stumped on how many colors to use in a room. While a monochromatic scheme (in which you select one color) may seem boring, you can add depth and interest by adding different intensities of that color, as well as lots of textures and patterns. For instance, a bedroom with light blue walls, a light blue comforter, light blue sheets, and light blue pillows cases may be boring. But a light blue room with a dark blue dust ruffle, a light blue comforter, striped blue and white sheets, and blue floral pillows cases can make a wonderful statement without involving other colors.

If monochromatic isn't your style, try using two or three complementary colors in a room, such as yellow walls with purple accents. Just be careful not to overdo it! Rooms with too many colors and patterns (unless you pull it off like an expert designer) can feel a little edgy.

Displaying Art

What exactly is art? The longer I search for a definition, the more elusive it seems to become. For many people, art (for the purposes of decorating a home environment) is a clear-cut proposition. It is often framed and is typically a painting, poster, or print of some sort that is hung on a wall. To others, art does not fit into this neat, structured definition. For them, art is anything they want to call art. In other words, a Picasso hanging on a wall is just as much art as a strip of hundred-year-old wood removed from a barn during demolition. Both can be hung on a wall and admired. So one is just as much art as the other, to those who believe art can be any thing of beauty displayed in your space.

In my *American Heritage Dictionary*, art has nine definitions. My favorite defines it as "human effort to imitate, supplement, alter, or counteract the work of nature." I love the idea that art "supplements" what exists around me. For me, this is what art truly does—adds to and enhances my environment.

The Art of Selecting Art

I've heard it many times from many different types of people. I've had friends ask me to come along when they shop for art because they don't feel they know how to pick out things that will look good in their homes. I usually go along, and they end up picking out all their own stuff. I'm just sort of the "artistic moral support" they think they need, but in truth, they don't need me at all.

If you think you aren't very good at selecting art work, think again. I mean really *think*. Haven't you ever walked into someone's home and *admired* their art? (Try to remember the style, and that might be a good one for you.) Then again, haven't you ever walked into someone's home and *hated* the art they had on their walls? (Remember that style and try to stay away from it.)

My home has lots of inexpensive folk art sprinkled around on the walls. Some people walk in and rave over it all. Others walk in and say, "Oh, nice to see you hang up your kids' artwork. It's . . . um . . . *nice*." Oh well, to each his own.

So when you set out to buy artwork for your apartment, whether you're off to the flea market, yard sales, discount stores, or wherever, try to remember these tips:

- **Color.** Try to find art that works with the color of your walls, furnishings, curtains, and other things in your apartment. Many of us have had a piece of art that just doesn't seem to go with anything we own, haven't we?

- **Size.** If you're trying to fill a particular space, measure it out before you go shopping.

- **Mood.** If it makes you smile right away and it's in your price range, it might be right for you. If it makes you nervous or edgy or inspires other not-so-desired emotions, keep looking. Don't buy a piece of art just because the salesperson thinks it's great or because you like the frame or the colors used. Buy art that speaks to you, especially when you like what it's saying.

- **Adaptability.** Try to purchase art that can be used in different rooms, so redecorating (by just rearranging) will always be an option for you.

- **Don't buy on impulse.** If at all possible, go home and think about it for a while. The only mistakes I've ever made in buying art happened when I bought on impulse. (However, if you're shopping at flea markets or yard sales, you'll have to forget this rule.)

- **Buy what you love.** Who cares if you think a velvet rendering of dogs shooting pool is the best art in the world? Buy what you love, and it *will* look great in your space.

Decorating With Architectural Pieces

Remember when people used to renovate a house and much of the debris would end up at the curb? Before Rachel Ashwell's "shabby chic" style burst onto the world in 1996, after the publication of her book by the same name, things like old mantels, ceiling tin, and other architectural pieces were often discarded for trash pickup, and most people would not have given them a second look as they drove on by (although many savvy decorators—pros and amateurs—have always kept their eye to the curb, looking for treasures). Today, shabby chic is still one of the hottest decorating trends around, and you'd have to fight off the budget decorators (and even interior designers) if you happened across such a pile. Architectural pieces are rare finds at the curb today, but they can now be found everywhere from flea markets to pricey antique shops, and the more battered the piece, the better.

If you're lucky enough to find architectural elements at a reasonable price (or even for free!), here are a few ways you can use them to decorate your apartment home:

◉ **Corbels.** Create a unique shelf by mounting two corbels to the wall and placing a wood or glass strip on top.

◉ **Mantels.** They're not always easy to find, but if you keep your eyes open, you may stumble across them. (They are abundant at some of the antiques flea markets I visit—ones that cater to dealers.) Although the prices may sometimes seem high for the tightest budgets (I've seen them from $65 to more than $1,000, but I find most fall in the low $100s), they can completely transform a room. Use larger ones as a headboard, and smaller ones as a creative focal point for a room that lacks detail.

- **Moldings.** Strips of deep crown molding make great shelves, perfect for propping framed art and displaying small trinkets.

- **Doorknobs.** Abundant at flea markets and typically very affordable, old doorknobs can be used to create plate racks, coat racks, and many other usable treasures. They're also beautiful in their own right. I once visited an antiques shop and saw a crystal bowl filled with crystal doorknobs used as the centerpiece on a formal table.

- **Ceiling tin.** Sheets of ceiling tin are available at reasonable prices (I've seen them as low as $15 for a twenty-four by twenty-eight-inch piece) on eBay, at salvage yards, and at flea markets. Get a pair of tin snippers, and you can use ceiling tin to create picture or mirror frames (snip out the middle section, insert art or a mirror, and secure wood backing). You can also create a very simple fireplace screen (slightly bend a square section, and it'll stand on its own). Some of the squares I find are so decorative, they look great just hanging on a wall all by themselves!

Creative Ways to Display Artwork

Displaying artwork may seem like a simple enough task. You find it, bring it home, choose the location, measure the area to find the right spot, and then secure a screw or nail into the wall. It's as easy as that, right? Well, that depends on what you really want. Yes, you certainly can follow traditional hanging methods, and you may be perfectly happy with the result. On the other hand, you may wish to approach hanging your art as something more—thinking of displaying art as something of an art in itself.

For instance, do you have a piece of artwork you love that you want to highlight in a special way? Try thinking beyond single pieces and instead consider creating an artistic grouping. If you have a Victorian-style print, how about grouping it with a few plates, tole trays, a small shelf, or a pair of sconces?

You should also carefully plan groupings and test them before you commit. Before you begin hanging the items, lay the entire grouping down on the floor, in the specific configuration you have in mind. See how the items work together, how the colors look, whether the group seems symmetrical or perhaps too narrow or too wide for the space you have to work with. The intent is to make your mistakes on the floor, not on your walls. Move items around until you have the perfect grouping on the floor, then get to work hanging it all up.

If you need inspiration or help to create a grouping, look around your apartment and try matching up different items until you have an arrangement that strikes your fancy. Groupings can include a few items with something in common, matching items, or completely separate items that have a theme or something that can tie them together and cause the grouping to make sense. For instance:

- ❖ Matched identical items could be a matched set of four framed vegetable prints in the same artistic style, in matching frames.
- ❖ Items with something in common could be a variety of family photos, all displayed in matching (but not necessarily identical) black frames.
- ❖ Separate items with a theme could be a rose print, a watering can, and a section of picket fencing—all different items that pertain to a garden theme.

Just Hanging Out

If you're out for a display method that's more interesting than the standard hang-it-on-a-nail method, try hanging your art in one of the following ways:

⚙ **Ribbon.** Suspend framed art from a ribbon for an elegant look.

⚙ **Removable adhesive hooks.** If you're worried about leaving holes in the wall, try using hanging aids that adhere to the wall with removable adhesive. I like the ones made with 3M's Command Adhesive.

⚙ **Lean it.** Pick up a decorating magazine these days and you're likely to see at least one photo layout that shows art-work (or photos, mirrors, and other such items) "leaning" instead of hanging. Try it by placing art on window ledges or on tables that are against a wall (see example in illustra-

Illustration 4-A. Pictures leaning on a window sill.

tion 4-A). Very large pieces look great right on the floor leaning against the wall. (You'll create no holes this way, and items are always easy to move when you're ready for a change!)

⚙ **Decorative hooks.** Instead of hanging art on a nail or screw, try something more decorative. Decorative drawer pulls are great, and they're especially attractive if you suspend the art from them on wire, twine, or ribbon. I find these at home decorating shops for just a few dollars a piece, in a wide range of styles, from colored glass to ceramic.

Decorating With Books

When I walk into a home that contains many books, I always get a cozy, comfortable feeling. I'm not sure what it is about books, exactly, that makes a space a little warmer, a little more "homey," but they always seem to do it.

Book collections also tell a lot about their owners. In keeping with my antique-inspired cottage theme, my book collection consists of battered old (but not valuable) volumes of Shakespeare and Dickens' tales. Not only are they wonderful to read, but they're wonderful to look at.

So if you have books in your home, why not take them off the bookshelves, dust them off, and put them to good use? Here are some ways to use books to decorate:

- Stack up large books on the floor and place a piece of glass or wood on top to create a small side table.

- Place small book stacks of varying heights on a table. Place framed photos, candlesticks, or other items on top of and around the books and you can achieve perfect height and balance.

- On an ottoman or coffee table, set out trays or baskets holding books so visitors can browse through them. This is especially nice if you have antique volumes, art books, or rare editions to share with your guests.

Rip It Out

Warning: If you're a devout bibliophile, my next suggestion might turn your stomach. If not, try this project: Hit a flea market or some yard sales. Pick a variety of books, preferably some with pictures. Get out your trusty utility knife and try the following:

- Cut out pages and use them to "wallpaper walls" or sections of walls by applying spray adhesive to the back of each page. If this is just too daring for you, try wallpapering an inexpensive section of wood (such as paneling) and propping it behind a desk.

- Remove pages and "wallpaper" the back of a bookcase.

❖ Use pages to decorate picture frames and bulletin boards.

❖ Decorate an old desk by gluing and decoupaging print and graphics pages; then add a polyurethane finish or a glass top to protect it and make it more usable.

Where to Find Art

Some of the places we've already discussed to shop for attractive furnishings are also great spots to find art:

❖ **Discount stores.** Discount stores not cool enough for you? You may be surprised. It might take some digging, but you're bound to find a few low-cost pieces of art that suit your taste. Look for prints you like—you can always embellish an existing frame or reframe the whole thing. Also try crafts stores like Michaels and Garden Ridge. Their prices are good, and their sales are great.

❖ **Yard sales and flea markets.** I've snatched up complete sets of four matching prints for as little as $10 at yard sales. If you're a flea market lover, you'll have even more to choose from.

❖ **Online stores.** Too busy to shop for art? No problem! Just log on to a few Web sites and shop whenever it's convenient for you, even if it's the middle of the night. Art.com (www.art.com) and Next Monet (www.nextmonet .com) have really nice collections for a variety of decorating styles.

❖ **A child's notebook.** When my daughter was seven, she came home from school with an incredible painting that reminded me of Keith Haring's pop art creations from the 1980s. I framed it and hung it on the wall and have received many compliments on this unique, modern-looking piece. Ask the children in your life (e.g., neighbors, nieces, and friends) about their latest creations.

❖ **Postcards and greeting cards.** No matter your style or interests, you can probably find some postcards or greeting cards that appeal to you. Buy a few, purchase inexpensive frames, and create a grouping or use them all by themselves. They're perfect for a hallway, stairwell, or other long, narrow spaces.

❖ **Calendars.** I have some friends who love the now-famous Blue Dog prints by the artist Rodrigue. But given the escalating cost of his work, one large framed print was the maximum for their budget. So I was surprised to see that their son's bedroom now has several framed Blue Dog prints, and I asked how they'd done it. Easy, they said–they purchased a Blue Dog calendar (for about $25), and when the year was over, they removed and framed several months' graphics. The result: six new prints, for just the small additional cost of very inexpensive frames. Plan ahead by purchasing calendars each year that have beautiful graphics you'd like to see hanging in your home the following year.

Creative Arrangements

Having a limited decorating budget is nothing more than an opportunity to be creative. So when you're facing a blank wall and trying to figure out the best way to fill it without busting your budget, remember your choices are not limited to artwork, shelves, or anything else that traditionally ends up on your walls. Think outside the box, keep your eyes wide open, and seek inspiration wherever you can find it. Try these simple projects to get you started:

- **An instant window.** If you have a wall that needs a window but doesn't have one, don't despair. Hang an old window right on the wall (I get used windows for $3 at flea markets), then mount a rod above it and hang a curtain around it just as if it were a real window.

- **Fun and functional.** Vintage or interesting new game boards (e.g., checkers, and backgammon) look great hanging on walls. When it's time for a game, just pull them down and play!

- **Nonart as art.** Gather a variety of old picture frames and display them sans the artwork. They also look great "layered" over a mirror or propped up on window sills or mantels.

A New Life for Old Windows, Doors, and Shutters

Windows, door, shutters—they're just parts of buildings, right? Correct, but they can be more. If you're lucky enough to live within driving distance of a salvage yard, this is the place to begin when looking for these items. (They'll likely be abundant and cheap there.) If you're not convenient to a salvage yard, check with flea markets and friends who are remodeling. Once you have your hands on a few choice pieces, there are many ways to use them in simple decorating projects.

Doors can be used to create the following:

❖ **Tables.** Use an old door as a table top. For instance, in a home office, two filing cabinets can act as your base and a door can serve as the surface. If the door is not completely flat, have a piece of glass cut to go on top. Personalize your desktop by placing family photos between the door and the glass.

❖ **Screen magic.** Old screen doors look great just propped up against a wall. Dress them up by hanging small framed art on them, or use them to display a hat collection. Pinning photos on the screen sections creates a sentimental conversation piece.

❖ **Privacy divider.** Hinge three doors together and create a "screen" or room divider (see example in illustration 4-B). This can also be used as a creative headboard.

Windows can also be used in a variety of creative, decorative ways. Pick up some used windows and try some of these quick and easy ideas:

❖ **Paint it.** Paint a base coat over the entire window, including the glass. Let it dry. Then break out the colors and paint a different picture on each square of glass— for example, a different kind of flower or geometric shape in each frame.

Illustration 4-B. Doors hinged together to create a room divider.

❖ **Wrap it up.** Paint the window frame, if desired. Secure the end of a long piece of rope or twine on the back on the window with a staple gun or tie it around a screw. Wrap the twine around the window until you have a nice geometric pattern. Slip photos, postcards, and other mementos behind the twine and hang it up.

❖ **Get hooked on it.** Paint the window frame with a creative design (e.g., stripes, polka dots), and add hooks (or old doorknobs) equally spaced on the bottom strip of the frame. Suspend on the wall, and you have a place to hang hats, coats, belts, jewelry, or whatever you like.

Shutters are wonderful, especially the kind with louvers that can still be opened and shut. Try these creative uses for them:

◉ Place a shutter on top of two pedestals or stools to create a sofa table.

◉ Hinge several small shutters together to create a fireplace screen or a computer monitor coverup.

◉ If your window lacks detail, hang shutters on each side of it (on the inside, that is) to create interest and instant architecture.

◉ For a garden theme, hang shutters on a wall and tuck seed packets and garden-theme postcards into the louvers.

Shelving

There was a time when some cinder blocks and a few strips of wood were very common materials for do-it-yourself shelving. The materials were cheap (if not free), anyone could put these items together, and the shelves were strong enough to hold a television set and stereo. If I had a dollar for every apartment I'd seen with one of these units in it (just during my college years!), I'd be one rich lady.

Another not-so-attractive (but often practical) trend in shelving involved acquiring plastic milk crates from the back of grocery stores (you can purchase them now at discount stores) and stacking them up. Although not as strong as the cinder-block-and-wood units, this type of makeshift shelf unit was (and still is) a favorite of teenagers and college students all over the country, thanks to its relative sturdiness and very low cost. (It's great for all those books!)

Most of the apartment dwellers I know today are a little older and ready for something a bit more sophisticated, even if their budget is low. So what can you do when you want grown-up style shelving on the cheap? Try some of these ideas:

- Find two ladders of equal height (new or used) and paint them as you wish. Place them parallel to each other, several feet apart. Purchase a few pieces of glass or wood. (Paint or stain the wood.) Rest each end of the glass or wood shelves on the corresponding ladder step, and you have a great, Country-style shelf unit.

- Conserve floor space by purchasing deep molding, cutting several pieces to the same width, and then attaching them to a wall—for instance, each one foot apart vertically. This is a great place to display framed art, candles, a doll collection, and trinkets.

- Scour yard sales for bookshelves that appear to be the right size for your needs. If you find one you like, bring it home, sand it a bit, and then apply a primer. From there, use one of the faux finishing techniques described earlier in this chapter.

Ideas, Tips, and Tricks

Painting:

- Instead of just painting a room (or a wall) a solid color, paint vertical stripes—just tape off sections and get to work. Or paint a room one color; then paint shiny stripes by adding strokes of clear glaze in vertical strips.

- When shopping for paint, don't forget to check the "Oops Shelf." This area holds paints that were incorrectly mixed, although someone else's Oops Paint might just be the perfect color for you. Oops Paint can normally be purchased at a big discount.

On your walls:

- Buy (wall-mount) mirrors in strips at home improvement stores and embellish them by gluing beads, silk flowers, buttons, plastic ivy, moss, or any interesting material around the edges.

- Look through your photo album and find pictures of interesting buildings, landscapes, or people that have an artsy look. Frame them, hang then up, and your photographic handiwork will be enjoyed much more often than if it's hidden in an album!

- Put together a collection or a collage of items in a shadow box frame, like vintage buttons, old stamps, or ticket stubs.

- Everyone needs a bulletin board somewhere, but it doesn't have to look like a bulletin board. Paint your board and frame with an interesting color that complements your room. Hang it from a wide, patterned ribbon and it looks more like art than a place to pin up coupons and invitations.

chapter 5

Windows

Think about the last time you were in a room without windows. What did it feel like? Did you feel somewhat trapped? Unable to breathe? As if you were choking?

Okay, maybe being without a window doesn't drive you to such extreme emotions. After all, so many of us who work in office buildings have no window near us throughout most of the day. In fact, having a view of the outside while you're working is considered a privilege, something many people actually aspire to. Hence the saying "window office"–and all the prestige that goes with it.

Luckily, you won't have to "earn" windows in your apartment; you'll probably have at least a few when you move in. And though the bare-window look is popular now (and really has always been), sometimes you want at least a little something besides glass between you and the world outside.

Window treatments come in an assortment of styles: valances, swags, curtains, draperies, miniblinds, roller shades, shutters, and many others. Some of these are attractive as well as utilitarian, while others are used for decorative purposes alone. What you choose to go over, around, or on your windows is up to you. But as you search through your options, remember your goals, and be sure to stay true to them!

No-Sew Window Treatments

I must admit, I have always felt a bit inferior because I lack a talent so many people, especially women, seem to have. Sometimes, I silently watch these people as they flaunt their talent, one that enables them to create fabulous things that people want, need, and use. The talent I lack is sewing. I can't sew anything except a crude hem, although I can reattach a button if one happens to come loose or fall off. Still, I always felt like my lack of sewing talent would keep me from partaking in something I wanted to do for many years—make my own window treatments. So I spent years purchasing premade curtains, believing I simply had to live with the fact that I needed to sew in order to tackle this type of decorating project.

Then one day at a crafts store, I was strolling along, and there it was. Beside me was a small, unassuming bottle of a mysterious potion called "fabric glue." "What? Can it be? Is it possible that with fabric, my scissors, and a bit of this stuff I could actually be allowed (even if just briefly) into the inner circle of crafters who can work with fabric?"

I quickly purchased the bottle of glue and then stopped at a fabric store on the way home. I purchased several yards of beautiful, clearance-rack fabric. I arrived home and cut the fabric into rectangular strips. I then carefully glued a small hem and folded over the top as well. This I glued also, but I left openings at the sides to create a pocket so I could slide in a curtain rod. The result nearly brought tears to my eyes—my new valances were beautiful. And I had made them all by myself.

Of course, I was quite embarrassed to learn that fabric glue has been around for a pretty long time, but I hadn't seen it because I'd never looked for it. But now that I'd found it, I felt like the weekend home fix-it folks when they first discovered duct tape: here's something that might not be the best solution, but it's a pretty darned good one!

Materials for No-Sew Treatments

Wonderful as fabric glue may be, I don't want you to think that's all you need for creating window treatments. You could probably get along just fine with fabric and this glue, but why get along just fine? You can do better than fine! And the answer lies in locating tools and materials that make creating no-sew window treatments as easy as it is fun:

- **Rods.** The great thing about plastic or aluminum window treatment rods is that they're inexpensive and you can find them at decorating, discount, and home improvement stores. Tension rods are great for rental apartments, because they don't require mounting on the wall and leave no holes. (They have a spring inside, and you simply push the two sides together, put it in place, and let it go—it stays put inside the frame.) Decorative rods are pricier but can add very dramatic effects to your windows.

- **Other hanging devices.** You're not limited to plain old rods for hanging treatments. Fallen branches are free (now that's cheap!) and can easily be trimmed down and used instead of a rod in garden, rustic, or nature-theme rooms. Decorative hooks or doorknobs hold up swags wonderfully.

- **Ribbons.** Ribbons can be used as drapery tiebacks. They can also be sewn to the top of a panel as tabs. And if you're really daring, forget the panel and just use the ribbons! Purchase a variety of many ribbons and cut them to the exact same length. Tie each one onto a rod and line them up, and you've created a whimsical ribbon valance (see example in illustration 5-A).

◎ **Fabric.** Your local fabric store and discount stores with a fabric department are always great places to check for window treatment materials.

◎ **Tablecloths.** I received some beautiful tablecloths as wedding gifts, but I rarely use them. (Since I have kids, placemats always seemed more practical.) So I turned them into curtains and get to enjoy them everyday, instead of just on special occasions! It's easy to add small hooks to hang a crochet tablecloth on a rod, and a linen tablecloth requires just a few hand-sewn-on ribbons so it can be suspended from a rod.

◎ **Napkins.** Cloth napkins are some of the most versatile items I have ever worked with on crafts projects. One great way to use cloth napkins is to hang a rod and fold several over the rod, side by side, points facing downward.

Illustration 5-A. An improvised ribbon valance.

◎ **Blankets and quilts.** Isn't it wonderful to cuddle up with a fleece blanket on a chilly night? Another nice thing about fleece is the price: Fleece blankets are amazingly affordable (throws are even under $20), incredibly soft, and come in a rainbow of hues. (Fleece is priced from $6 to $15 per yard at my local fabric store.) Try making a fleece window treatment by folding or suspending a fleece throw over a rod. Quilts make great, Country-style curtains, too, but they tend to be a bit heavier, so be sure you have a sturdy rod in place to hold them.

⊚ **Creative alternatives.** Who needs curtains? Hang things in your windows that you love, like drying herbs or vintage utensils hanging from twine.

⊚ **Embellishments.** Let's say you've created a valance with cloth napkins like the one I described earlier. If you add a pom-pom at the end of each point, you've created a wonderful, Harlequin-style valance for just a few dollars! Also use beads, tassels, buttons, stencils, paints, and other inexpensive supplies to dress up your homemade, no-sew window treatments.

A New Life for Sheets

Sheets never struck me as being very exciting. Since I love patterned comforters and quilts, I always opted for boring, solid-color sheets to reduce clash potential. To tell you the truth, I really never gave sheets much thought—that is, until I encountered a problem in my dining room several years ago.

I went a little crazy one afternoon and decided I needed one formally decorated room. I bought a deep, red paint and painted the entire room with it. Then I tricked my mother out of a fabulous, formal painting to hang in the room. (She was ready to give it up, really, she was.) After painting the room, I stenciled a fleur-de-lis design in metallic gold under the chair rail and filled my glass-front china cabinet with all my wedding china (a formal Noritake pattern) and crystal. The look was formal and fabulous. Then, I looked at my windows. "Oh, no, what am I going to do here?" I went shopping and confirmed something I'd always suspected: that formal draperies can be very expensive. I found several gorgeous curtains, such as thick velvet panels

and others made from a shimmering, metallic silk. But all were far beyond my price range, with some as high as $250 per panel.

Then, as I was going to bed that night, I noticed something. My queen-size sheets seemed to be just about the same length as a curtain panel. The next morning, I hit a store that carries a huge variety of slightly irregular linens. I found four flat sheets (twin size were just the right width) and purchased them for a painless total of $8. I took them home, spread them out on the kitchen floor, and anchored the corners with stacks of books. I used the fleur-de-lis stencil and gold paint I'd used on the dining room walls and decorated the deep taupe sheets with the same design. I slipped a rod into the top (no sewing, just a few scissors snips to open the top hem and insert the rod), and my dining room had personalized draperies for less than $10 per window.

Sheets can be used for lots of fun, inexpensive decorating projects. Try these simple ideas:

❖ Buy an extra flat sheet that matches your bed linens, and use the sheet as a curtain panel or turn it into a valance.

❖ In addition to paint and stencils, use the following to decorate your sheets and help them grow up into curtains: paint markers, beads, tassels, buttons, and rubber stamps with ink.

❖ Purchase no-sew cornice or valance kits and use an inexpensive sheet with them, instead of pricey fabric.

❖ Sew two flat sheets together on three sides, and attach buttons, hooks, or Velcro on the fourth side. Voilà, you have a custom-made duvet cover.

❖ Pair a flat sheet with a liner to create a simple, inexpensive shower curtain.

Sewing-Required Window Treatments

So you can sew, eh? Wow! You have my undying admiration and maybe even my occasional envy (like when I need a new duvet cover). You are in a wonderful position to create beautiful window treatments. But first, you need ideas.

Finding Patterns and Ideas

Where do you find inspiration for window treatments? My sewing friends suggest:

- Decorating books and magazines

- Samples on display in fabric stores

- Pattern books

- The homes of family, friends, and acquaintances

Okay, let's say you're an experienced sewer and you need patterns but are tired of pattern books. Why not create your own patterns? Try drawing out your own patterns on packing paper. You can try to wing it and create your own design, if you're really confident, or you could get help from an "inspiration piece." For instance, if a neighbor has a window treatment you love, ask if you can take it down for a few hours and use it as a guide for your own pattern.

You can also vary an existing pattern or combine patterns. One sewer recently explained that she had a pattern that was almost perfect, but she really wanted some unique tab tops on it. She found a pattern with just such tabs and combined the two patterns to achieve the one she wanted but could not find ready-made.

Also check your local fabric store for classes. It's a great place to meet other sewers and swap ideas.

Basic Window Treatments

Here are some ideas to sew in a limited time:

❖ **Valances.** Purchase fabric, cut into lengths, and fold. Sew a straight stitch a few inches from the top, then another above it, leaving a space for a rod pocket. To make it more formal, drape cording or tassels on the valance.

❖ **Tab-top curtains.** Take one length of material, fold over the top and bottom hems, and iron. Stitch the hems and add tabs made from coordinating ribbon (see example in illustration 5-B).

If you're serious about sewing your own window treatments, try purchasing a book on the subject. *How to Dress a Naked Window* by Donna Babylon has more than thirty window treatment ideas with complete instructions that even an amateur (like me!) can understand.

Illustration 5-B. Tab-top curtain hanging from a window frame.

Blinds and Shades

Plastic or aluminum miniblinds are standard issue for many rental apartments. But if you have a room with bare windows in places where you need privacy, purchasing and installing your own miniblinds is easy and quite inexpensive. The drawback to purchasing blinds (or shades) for a rental is that when it's time to move out and you take them with you, they may not fit your new place's windows.

If, however, you own your place or you're planning to stay in your apartment for a while, miniblinds are easy to install and use, sturdy, come in a variety of colors, and are excellent for providing privacy.

Roller shades are also a great choice when privacy is a concern. However, I have noticed that plain, white roller shades can be a little boring. But there are many ways to dress them up and make them more attractive and less institutional, such as the following:

- ❧ **Con-Tact paper or wallpaper.** Con-Tact paper is great because you can just peel and stick it onto your shade. Wallpaper and wallpaper borders can also be applied to shades to coordinate with your room or just to add color and a design.

- ❧ **Paint.** Acrylic paints are great for personalizing roller shades and adding colors that coordinate perfectly with your decor. Paint markers offer even better control for those who feel less artistic or less confident handling a paintbrush.

- ❧ **Stamps.** Check your local crafts store for stamps made of rubber or foam. Look for those that have designs that aren't very small and intricate, so the design is clear even at a distance. (Tip: Try foam stamps designed for stamping on walls.)

Ideas, Tips, and Tricks

- ❧ Line up a series of glass bottles (in various colors) on a window sill and watch the light dance through them.

- ❧ Instead of traditional, matching tiebacks, use ribbon, twine, raffia, or wire strung with colorful beads.

❖ Lace panels and sheers let the sunlight enter a room in a light, airy way.

❖ Place large plants in front of windows for privacy without a window treatment.

❖ At fabric stores, be sure to check out the remnant table. You can often find up to six or seven yards at huge discounts, and that's more than enough for a couple of valances or swags.

Unique Ways to Block an Unattractive View

Perhaps you have a wonderful view from every window in your apartment. Perhaps you see a distant cityscape or a rolling green meadow. Perhaps you are so happy with your views that you don't even worry about window coverings.

But then again, perhaps your views aren't quite so perfect. Looking out a window and seeing a less-than-attractive site is a common occurrence for apartment dwellers just about everywhere. And if your window treatment budget is tight or if you're a short-term renter, making an investment in something unique and spectacular may seem out of reach for you. But it doesn't have to be. And if valances, blinds, draperies, and other old standbys just don't seem creative enough for you, you don't have to stick with them. Consider these ideas:

◉ **Stained glass.** When you think of low-budget ways to dress your windows, perhaps stained glass isn't the first thing that comes to mind. But an old stained glass window can be suspended by wire or chains in front of your window (see example in illustration 5-C) or even propped up on a window sill. Sure, you could opt for blinds, but you may be surprised at what one stained glass window can do for a room. (It may even become your focal point.) If you have one window that catches beams of morning or afternoon sunlight, imagine what it will look like from the inside of your apartment as light streams through the sections of colored glass! If you're worried about the expense, here's something that may surprise you: I've picked up small to medium sized, antique stained glass windows at flea markets for as little at $40. (You can also find them on Internet auction sites like TIAS: www.tias.com.)

⊚ **Cling-on decals.** On a recent trip to Home Depot, I found something called Wallpaper for Windows (by Etch Art). It stays on your window thanks to static cling qualities, and it has the look of etched glass. You can put it up, clean it. and just peel it off when you're ready to move. (And it's very affordable.)

⊚ **Glass frosting.** Use glass frosting spray (be sure to properly ventilate the area while you work) to create a design on your window that lets the light in but provides some (but not always absolute) privacy. Stick lace (with spray adhesive) or tape a stencil onto the window, and then spray the glass frosting solution directly onto it. (It may require several coats.) You can still clean your window without damaging the design, but you can also remove it with a razor blade if you change your mind or move out.

Illustration 5-C. Stained glass window suspended from chains in front of window.

chapter **6**

Furniture

When you found your apartment, you probably toured the inside when it was completely empty. Do you remember what it felt like? Sure, it was important for you to see the exact size of each room, the condition of the flooring, and other such details. But chances are, you didn't feel like you were looking at a "home." But then, after you moved in your furniture and other belongings, it began to feel like a home, didn't it? Hopefully, it did.

Try as you may, but it might just be impossible to overestimate the importance of your furniture. Stop and recall, for a moment, the really "bad" furniture you've encountered in your life. Think about the times you've slept on an uncomfortable guest bed, for example—the kind with a spring poking into your back all night long. Or the couch at your great-aunt's house that she's had covered in plastic for the past twenty years, the kind you stick to and have to peel yourself from when you stand up. Now, think about the good furniture you've had the pleasure of knowing in your life. For me, the perfect example is a floral fabric-upholstered chair in my childhood bedroom. The back and seat were stuffed with down feathers, and I would literally sink into it and read, write, talk on the phone, and daydream. It was the most heavenly spot in the world to me, and that was mostly because of the way that chair felt, as if it were embracing me with security and comfort.

Do you have (or have you ever had) such a perfect piece of furniture? A bed with a mattress that was not too soft, not too hard, but just right? A recliner in your living room that's so comfortable you sneak naps in it every chance you get? If so, then you know how I felt about my feather-stuffed chair.

New Furniture

You may remember a time when furniture was just, well, furniture. Perhaps you can even remember the way your parents bought furniture years ago. If the family needed a dining room table, for instance, Mom and Dad would typically go down to a local furniture store (perhaps one owned by a family friend or neighbor), pick one out that fit the family and looked nice and seemed sturdy, and that was that. But today furniture buying seems to be more complicated, perhaps because our lives are more complicated. Because of the huge selection available to us in our consumer-driven society, we can find furniture that precisely suits our lifestyles and our tastes. Flea markets, consignment shops, and garage sales have made it possible for us to reuse resources in yet another way, by helping us purchase previously owned furniture so we can recycle it and give it a new life. What was once a "throwaway" sofa may be transformed into a prized piece with little more than a slipcover. And new furniture isn't just found in furniture stores anymore. You can now purchase new furniture at discount stores and membership warehouses, from catalogs, and via the Internet.

Something Old, Something New

As much as I extol the virtues of recycling used furniture to keep decorating costs down, I must admit, some pieces are best purchased new, such as mattresses. It's also wise to purchase new (or relatively new) baby cribs and other children's furniture, to assure they meet current safety standards.

I confess, I searched for a previously owned sofa for years until finally giving up and purchasing a new one. In addition, many budget decorators just love the look and feel of new furniture, and we should all have things that we love in our homes. But you may be asking, "If I have a very limited budget, will I ever get new furniture? Am I destined to live with my parents' hand-me-downs forever?" Of course not! There's plenty of affordable new furniture out there. You just have to know where to look. Some of the best places to look include the following:

⊚ **Outlet centers.** I had a burning desire for a sofa from Storehouse Furniture that went unfilled for years due to my limited budget—that is, until I located their outlet center in a town nearby. There, in the clearance room, I located a large, comfortable sofa in the perfect color, discounted substantially because of a small defect on the back. (I never even fixed it because the defect is up against the wall!) So if you find something you love at a furniture store but it's out of your price range, don't give up just yet. Check your local telephone directory, check the Internet, and ask around. You might just find an outlet store near you with the very same piece for less, or you may be able to buy the piece directly from the manufacturer.

⊚ **Warehouse stores.** If you only head to Costco and Sam's Club for groceries, you might be missing out! Membership-required warehouse stores often carry some furniture and home accessories, often at big discounts over retail stores. The drawback: If you love it, be prepared to buy it immediately. Once they run out, they might never get it back in stock again.

⊚ **Furniture stores.** Of course, it's logical that you would try shopping for new furniture at furniture stores. But what I want to offer is some "hows" of furniture store shopping. First, make sure you know when the sales hit. Often, salespeople can tell you when their store traditionally holds sales and what types of items are usually marked down. Obviously, the best time to shop for bargains is when these stores have tent sales and other specials. But all sales may not be advertised, so be sure to ask to be put on a store's mailing list if you're in the market for more new furniture. Also check your Sunday paper for stores that are going out of business or moving. And no matter where you shop for new furniture, always try to bargain, at least a little. I never knew this could be done until I watched my husband bargain $50 off a sofa that was already on sale at a store that's part of a well-known, national chain.

⊙ **Unfinished-wood stores.** It might sound like too much trouble. But then again, it's a good way to end up with furniture with the *exact* paint color or stain you want. (See "Wood Furniture Painting Tip" sidebar on page 114.) Another great thing about unfinished furniture stores is that many will do custom pieces for you at no extra cost, so you can get precisely what you want at a decent price.

Don't Throw It Away!
Making Treasures from Would-Be Trash

Every year, Americans throw away more and more tons of trash. Much of the trash you produce may truly be garbage. But what if some of it isn't garbage at all? What if some of the broken, unwanted, or seemingly unusable things you toss into your garbage can could be used to create one-of-a-kind, low-cost (or no-cost) decorative touches in your home?

The idea of turning trash to treasure has really come into vogue in recent years. Many books and magazine articles on the topic have been published, and several television shows are being produced that highlight trash-to-treasure projects. Want to join in on the trend? Here are some simple ideas to get you started:

- **Steel or metal cans.** Remove labels, punch holes through the walls in a pattern (such as a star or a heart), and use them as indoor or outdoor candle-holding luminaries.

- **Outgrown (kids') clothing.** Frame infant clothing in a shadowbox and hang it on your wall as a prized memento.

- **Old blankets.** Use old blankets to re-cover throw pillows.

- **Damaged books.** Remove and frame illustrations, and you have inexpensive wall art; rip out text pages and use them to decoupage furniture, such as the top of a writing desk or the back of a bookcase.

- **Damaged sofas or chairs.** Cover the most terribly stained or even ripped sofa or chair with a slipcover. If premade slipcovers are too pricey for your budget, try covering furniture with bed sheets—just tuck and pin the fabric until you've covered all the surfaces.

- **Broken china.** Smash it to bits and use the pieces to create a mosaic tabletop.

- **Candle wax remnants.** Melt down what's left when you have a few collected, and create new candles with them. Just pour into a small jar and add a wick.

- **Baby food jars.** Decorate them to hold small items (e.g., safety pins), or use them as votive candle holders by embellishing the outside with paint markers.

New Furniture Selection

If you're shelling out your hard-earned money for new furniture, be sure you buy wisely! Once again, look over your decorating goals statement and review your budget. Determine what style of furniture you're hoping to find, and have a figure in mind for what you'd like to spend. Hit a few furniture stores (preferably those in the midst of big sales!), and begin looking. Also consider the following advice for new furniture shopping:

- **Keep it neutral.** A few interior designers I know urge customers to purchase large items, such as sofas, in neutral colors. With these neutral backdrops in place, accent colors can be added with accessories, pillows, rugs, and curtains.

- **Check upholstery options.** Just because it's on the showroom floor in green chenille doesn't mean you can't buy it in white damask. Ask the salesperson if the sofa or chair that's caught your eye comes in other colors or patterns. Be sure to ask for the price difference (higher or lower) *before* you place your order.

- **Test it out, and test it some more.** Don't be shy about testing out your furniture while it's still in the store. Sit on it, lie on it, rub your hands over the upholstery and see how it feels. If you have a partner, children, or a roommate, take them along and let them try out pieces you're thinking about purchasing. (It's better than hearing complaints later!)

- **Cover it up.** You've found the almost perfect sofa. It's the perfect size, the perfect shape, and it's more comfortable that anything you've ever sat on in your life. Oh, there is one problem—its upholstery is bright orange. But it is also on clearance, and the markdown is huge. Do you give up and go home? No! You snatch it up and find a sale-rack slipcover in the perfect shade at a nearby fabric store. (Slipcovers aren't just for used furniture.)

Furniture Specifics

Okay, so you need furniture, and lots of it. Perhaps you're just starting out and this is your first apartment. Or maybe you've just moved to a larger place, and your belongings have lots of air between them now. Or perhaps you're just ready for a new look. No matter the reason, there are many places to find furniture and many ways to improve used pieces, particularly if you're willing to do a little work with less than ideal pieces. Consider these ideas:

- ❖ **Couches.** Pick up the comfiest you can find at garage sales. You can throw a slipcover on it or even cover it with a quilt.

- ❖ **Coffee tables.** An unattractive wood stain can be white-washed with paint that's thinned with water for a cottage look. Or instead of a coffee table, try two large footstools side by side. (Find them secondhand and recover them.)

- ❖ **Desks.** Two filing cabinets with a door, piece of wood, or strip of glass on top becomes a makeshift desk that can last for years. Want to make it a bit more fun? Paint the filing cabinets with a funky design. Or pick up any old dining table at a flea market, paint it, and add a keyboard drawer for better ergonomics, if you'll be using it for computer work.

- ❖ **CD and videotape holders.** Stack a few wooden crates, old soda cases, or vintage wine boxes to store all your CDs and videotapes.

❖ **Dining set.** Add slipcovers to folding metal chairs and throw a tablecloth (or even a quilt) over a folding card table.

Wood Furniture Painting Tip

If you're working with unfinished furniture, it's easy to create a great-looking, personalized piece with the paint color of your choice. Simply sand the surface, if necessary, and then apply a primer as a base coat, a top coat, and a varnish on top, if desired.

Working with water-based paint is best, particularly if the furniture is for kids, according to Liz Carter, co-owner of a Georgia-based home decorating shop that specializes in hand-painted furniture. Carter says water-based paints are safer than those with an oil base, they dry quickly, and they carry no odor.

Liz Carter and Catherine Garner are co-owners of The Purple Cow, in Marietta, Georgia. (See the Resources in the back of this book for contact information.)

Reviving Used and Old Furniture

When I find a piece of used furniture—whether it's an antique or just a few years old—that has potential, I feel a tingle of joy. My mind races through my repertoire of ideas for creative ways to bring it back to life, enhance it, or improve it. Many people I know feel the same way. Hunting for the perfect piece and finding a way to turn an ugly duckling into a beautiful swan is satisfying and fun. It has become so popular that many flea markets are seeing their attendance numbers grow and grow. And people who host frequent yard sales tell me their furniture is always "the first to go."

There are many benefits to buying used and old furniture for your home:

- **Environmental sense.** Given the deteriorating state of our planet, recycling on every level is important. Picking up a previously owned desk or bookshelf may not seem like an environment-saving act, but it's just as conscientious as hauling your aluminum and newspaper to the neighborhood recycling center. The more you recycle, the more responsibly you are using resources, the more you'll save, and the better you'll feel.

- **The test of time.** If you find a thirty-year-old chair that is sturdy and solid, you've found a piece that has stood the test of time and survived.

- **Courage to experiment.** Say you find a nice little writing desk in an atrocious color at a yard sale. No problem! When you only pay $10 for it, you can paint it, repaint it, and do whatever you like with it. Even big mistakes won't hurt as much when your capital outlay is so small.

Cleaning Old Furniture

My parents had several pieces of antique furniture in their home when I was growing up. I particularly liked a china hutch, a Country-style piece made of walnut. My mother would dust it, wax it, and clean it often with commercial cleaning products.

Then sometime around my late teens, I began to notice something strange happening to the china hutch. It seemed to have developed a "film" that covered the entire piece. It was so thick I could actually take my fingernail and scratch through it, and some of the film would come off under my nail. Today, twenty years later, the film has turned into a heavy, sticky layer of residue, and the piece is not nearly as beautiful as it once was.

The moral of this story is, while you should read your cleaning labels carefully, that may not be enough! Although my mother probably followed the instructions on the product bottles, the hutch's condition grew worse and worse. So what can you do? The answer may be to go a little lighter and more natural, according to a suburban Atlanta-area antiques dealer.

Mary Kearney's Kennesaw, Georgia–based antiques shop is filled with beautiful wood furnishings and accessories of all kinds. I wondered how she kept all her pieces looking so great, and she offered a few tips:

* Use linseed or olive oil to shine up wood, instead of harsh commercial polishes. Of the commercial products available, she recommends Olde English.

* Opt for products made from natural products, like those containing citrus ingredients.

"But what about my mother's hutch—can it ever look great again?" I asked. Kearney said she thought there might be hope for that piece. For antiques with a sticky residue, she suggests cleaning with mineral spirits, which often can repair some of the damage. Thicker residues may even require a little light sanding.

Mary Kearney is an antiques dealer in suburban Atlanta.

It's Not What You Think

One day, I was visiting a friend who has a knack for creative decorating. I was admiring her beautiful new settee, when I realized it wasn't a settee at all. She'd taken an old crib, removed one side, and added pillows and cushions to make a unique, low-budget seating area (see example in illustration 6-A). Her ability to look beyond the crib and see something more is a talent we could all use, as we embark on our decorating adventures.

As a budget decorator on a quest to decorate your apartment, let this be your mantra: *I will not be tied to the traditional use of things.* Say it to yourself often—in the morning, in the evening, in the afternoon. But most of all, say it to yourself when you are out shopping. When you pick up something you love at the flea market and you're tempted to say, "But I don't need a big porcelain bowl," don't think of it that way. Realize that, of course, you don't need a porcelain bowl, but you may desperately need something to hold your collection of Western belts. The porcelain bowl then becomes not only something you love but something you can use wisely in your home.

Illustration 6-A. A settee made from an old crib, covered in pillows.

Some other nontraditional use ideas:

❖ Stack two or three wide benches to create a bookcase.

Illustration 6-B. Two garden urns with a door on top.

❖ Hang a ladder (not the folding kind—the old-fashioned ones with just one side) on a wall vertically, and it becomes a tall bookshelf; hang it horizontally, and it can hold quilts or blankets.

❖ Stack up old suitcases, and they can serve as an end table as well as storage area.

❖ Use an interesting chair as an end table, or hang it on a wall and use it as a shelf.

❖ Place two large garden urns a few feet apart, add a table top (e.g., glass or wood), and you have a great table or desk (see example in illustration 6-B).

❖ Use a shiny aluminum trash can as a table base.

Ideas, Tips, and Tricks

◉ Know your furniture brands. If you always seem to love pieces from a specific furniture manufacturer, make note of it. Check with buying clubs, Internet sites, designers, and anyone else who might know of places that carry your preferred brands for less.

◉ Whenever you find used furniture, be sure to clean it thoroughly and test out its strength before you put it to use.

Ten Ways to Dress Up a Chair

When I set out for a day of flea market or junk store shopping, I never quite know what I'll find. But there's one item I am almost certain I will come across at some point during the day—wooden chairs. If they're sturdy (try sitting on them and shifting your weight around a bit) and inexpensive (sometimes as little as $5), I always grab them. They're functional and easy to recycle.

If you're looking for ways to bring a wooden chair back to life, try these simple tactics:

1. **Paint.** Skip the stripping if you'd like. Just clean the surface thoroughly, sand it carefully, them prime and paint. A few hours later, your junk store chair is as good as new.

2. **Pad.** A pretty, soft chair pad makes a hard wooden chair a lovely place to rest.

3. **Netting.** Take a strip of netting a few yards wide and about two feet deep. Wrap around the back of the chair and secure into a bow or cinch with a decorative pin or silk flower. Drape the netting on the floor and you have a romantic chair that's perfect for a bathroom or paired with a vanity table.

4. **Beads.** Glue wooden beads in the colors of your choice along the top, along the bottom, and even up the sides of a chair for a funky look.

5. **Decoupage.** Use photos, postcards, stickers, or any kind of beautiful paper, glue it on the chair, and coat with a decoupage solution.

6. **Whitewash.** This technique works well with wooden chairs that are stained. Just thin out some latex paint and brush on lightly, letting some of the stain show through for a rustic, country cottage look. Lightly sand painted areas if you want more stain to show through.

7. **Makeshift slipcover.** Take a length of fabric or a sheet, drape it over the chair, and secure it into place by tying ribbons in various places. (You may need to cut some holes in the fabric to tie it very securely.)

8. **Ivy.** Wrap and glue plastic ivy on the sections of the chair where it won't interfere with comfortable sitting.

9. **Ribbons.** Tie or glue ribbons on legs and other areas for a storybook effect.

10. **Rubber stamps or stencils.** Clean, prime, and paint the chair, and then use stencils or rubber stamps to create texture by adding an interesting pattern.

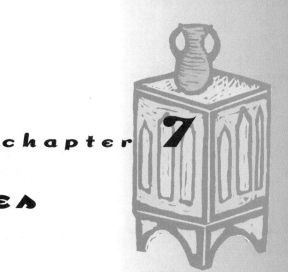

chapter 7

Accessories

Try to picture a room that has no accessories—nothing more than the necessary furnishings. While it may be a perfectly usable room, perhaps even pleasant in a streamlined, minimalist sort of way, it probably seems like it *lacks* something. Maybe it even feels the slightest bit cool and uninviting.

Accessories have a wonderful way of warming up a room and bringing it to life. They are frequently the conversation pieces that people notice most often in your home. In addition to their aesthetic appeal, some accessories also have a strong emotional appeal because of the memories tied up in them. For instance, when visitors admire a lovely porcelain vase in your living room, they may comment on its beautiful colors or unique shape. But to you, it may be an item you searched for high and low in a Paris flea market, hand in hand with the man who had just proposed marriage to you. A grouping of old family photographs may be interesting for visitors to examine, but to you, that grouping might include the only pictures you have of a favorite aunt who passed away long ago.

No matter what kinds of accessories you have in your home, remember to go for quality above quantity. Rooms crowded with meaningless knick knacks not only look busy, but they keep you busy (with all that dusting!) and give a room a cluttered look. But selecting a few items that you really love will add character and beauty to any room in your apartment.

Displaying Collections

Many people today have hopped on the "collecting" bandwagon, probably because collecting can be such an enjoyable hobby. My own collections include folk art, old books, and teacups with rose patterns. My brother has collected antique maps for years, and my friend Tim, a successful commercial director, has an impressive assortment of vintage cameras.

Illustration 7-A. An attractive display of grouped books.

For the people who have collections, hunting for and locating additions is nothing less than a thrill. But what happens when you arrive home with your treasure? Where will you put it, and how can you display your entire collection so that you (and your visitors) can enjoy it? You can display collections with the items either grouped or distributed throughout the home. Let's take a look at the positive and negative aspects of both:

❖ **Grouped.** If you'd like your collection to be viewed as a whole, keeping it together as a group is a good display choice (see example in illustration 7-A). This method works well when your collection has items that rely on one another to make sense. For instance, let's say you have a complete set of Shakespeare's works. If you place a volume or two in each room, the fact that you have a complete set may be lost. Likewise, military memorabilia, postage stamps, and political buttons might make more sense if displayed as a single, or just a few, groupings.

❖ **Distributed.** Although it may not be best for displaying a complete set of Shakespeare, distributing some collections to various rooms can work for many reasons. A contemporary art collector, for example, may have too many pieces (and some may be too large) to create a single grouping for display in any one room. But with two or three pieces in each room, the collection might show even better. This way, each room gets a boost of the color and a sampling from the collection. Antiques and other types of art collections also lend themselves well to being displayed in various rooms, for similar reasons.

Creative Display Techniques

If setting out a collection on a table or shelf just doesn't seem creative enough for you, there are many ways to create unique, cost-conscious displays. Here are some possibilities:

❖ **Window shelves.** For items such as colored glass bottles, place glass shelves in a window and line up the bottles. Eliminate your window treatment, and you'll be able to enjoy sunlight dancing through each color to create a spectacular show.

❖ **Baskets.** Is there anything that doesn't look great in baskets? Use baskets to hold everything from baseball caps to books to ethnic rug collections.

❖ **Shadow boxes.** If you have a collection of old jewelry, movie ticket stubs, keys, postcards, or anything that doesn't have a lot of physical depth, try pinning or otherwise attaching these items to backing (e.g., velvet) and hanging them on the wall in a shadow box frame for all to enjoy.

❖ **Bowls.** A silver or crystal bowl is a terrific way (though perhaps not an obvious one) to display a Native American belt or beaded necklace collection.

❖ **Molding shelves.** You can buy them premade or make your own (just buy molding at a home improvement or building supplies store). These shelves are sleek and unobtrusive, and you can place them high on your wall out of the way for delicate collections, such as breakable figurines.

❖ **Humorous displays.** Even if you're a serious collector, you don't need to have a serious display! Try inserting a little humor into your collection display, such as hanging your garden tool collection on a homemade scarecrow (see example in illustration 7-B) or displaying your travel memorabilia in an old suitcase.

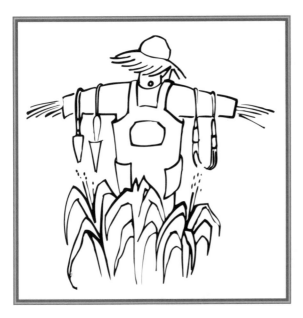

Illustration 7-B. Homemade scarecrow holding a garden tool collection.

Ten Great Uses for a Wicker Basket

Baskets are some of the most versatile, decorative, and useful items you can use in your home decorating. They come in a large assortment of sizes, shapes, and colors and can be picked up at a reasonable price everywhere from discount stores to home decorating outlets.

You can put your baskets to good use by looking around your apartment and deciding what items would look great contained in wicker baskets. Some ideas for wicker basket use include the following:

1. **Storing toys.** Use large baskets for bigger toys and small ones for things like cards and game pieces. Also keep them low so kids can easily retrieve and return toys.

2. **Trash cans.** Try an inexpensive basket instead of a plastic trash can in every room.

3. **Cooking utensils.** Place your often-used cooking utensils in attractive baskets right on your kitchen counter for a decorative touch and easy access to tools. (Keep the baskets fairly tall so utensils don't fall out.)

4. **Correspondence.** Create incoming and outgoing correspondence baskets so mail doesn't scatter.

5. **Periodicals.** Place newspapers and magazines in rectangular wicker baskets and situate them strategically where these periodicals are typically read.

6. **Food.** Keep bread, fruit, and other edibles in baskets on your counters or kitchen table.

7. **Clothing and accessories.** Large baskets can catch clothes that need to be laundered, while small to medium-sized baskets keep collections of scarves and belts tidy.

8. **Books.** You know all those awkward little books you have lying around, like software manuals and appliance instructions? Keep them in baskets, and you can slide them right onto a bookshelf. They'll be accessible when you need them but won't create an eyesore.

9. **Crafting supplies.** Arrange paper, paints, rubber stamps, knitting tools, and other crafting supplies in baskets with handles so you can pick them up and move them to the crafting location of your choice whenever you feel inspired.

10. **Office supplies.** Control home office clutter by storing office supplies (and even files) in a variety of decorative baskets.

A New Life for Ladders

I started seeing ladders popping up in decorating magazines a few years ago. First, it was the antique ones (with just one side, the kind you lean against a wall) that seemed to be getting popular. Now, even new ladders are getting the attention of amateur and professional decorators. The wood kind can be easily painted, and the aluminum kind have a sleek look that goes wonderfully with Contemporary furnishings.

If you're wondering how in the world you can use ladders in your own home, try using them as:

- A shelf unit for small or flat items, such as framed photos
- The side supports for home-made bookshelves
- A display for a variety of potted plants
- A nightstand or side table (the smaller ones)
- The base for a table (two small ladders plus a hard top surface)
- A display rack for fabric, blankets, or quilts by hanging the ladder horizontally on a wall (see example in illustration 7-C).

Illustration 7-C. Ladder turned into a display rack for fabric, blankets, or quilts.

Lighting

I once lived in a 1970s-style apartment that seemed to only reflect the worst decorating mistakes of that era. The lighting fixtures were truly the most horrendous I'd ever seen. The kitchen was worst of all, sporting two large, fluorescent lighting tubes. The light was so bright, it bothered almost everyone ever subjected to it, and it sent my guests wincing out of my kitchen the moment it was flipped on.

Other lighting fiascoes may include fixtures that are outdated or of poor quality so that they can break easily, clash with the other elements of the room, are too small or too large for a room, and, of course, those that are just plain ugly.

If you live in a rental, you may not be willing to invest in new lighting fixtures. But you can draw less attention to them by not using them very often. No, I am not suggesting that you live in darkness! But if you put a lamp or two in each room where the offending fixtures live, you can easily reduce their use. For instance, if you have two lamps with sixty- or hundred-watt bulbs, you might only rarely need your overhead light. You also have other creative lighting options, such as strip lighting that attaches under kitchen cabinets.

You can find lamps at discount stores, yard sales, and flea markets. But often, some of the lamps you will find there could use a bit of a facelift. Some ways to do that include:

❖ Painting the base a new color (or several new colors)

❖ Adding a new shade

Illustration 7-D. A lampshade that's been embellished with flowers.

❖ Embellishing a shade with anything from feathers to buttons to fringe to silk flowers (see example in illustration 7-D)

Accessories With a Purpose

Sure, lots of accessories are nice to look at. But what about the ones that look great *and* are functional? It doesn't get much better than that.

Accessories can serve many different types of purposes in your home:

- **Organizing and storage.** This can include baskets and bowls for storing large and small items; chalkboards and bulletin boards to help you keep your life organized; and crystal and porcelain knobs (instead of hooks) for hanging clothing, necklaces, belts, and other items.

- **Mirrors.** They're great-looking accessories that let you check your appearance and can also reflect light to help brighten a room.

- **Pillows.** They can inject a color or mood into a room and enhance the look of your sofa and chairs. (They're also great for naps!)

Purely Decorative Accessories

When it comes to accessories, some items are just attractive or interesting, even though they serve no purpose at all. These are the items we choose because when we saw them, we simply loved them, even if there was no rhyme or reason to that love.

A few years ago, I found a plastic, blow-up figure inspired by Edvard Munch's painting "The Scream." It's a quirky figure, and it goes with nothing in my home. I knew this, of course, as I slapped down $15 for it. But something about it spoke to me, so I bought it without thinking through the logic of this purchase. The plastic figure currently sits atop a mahogany armoire, and I don't plan to give it up, ever.

Purely decorative accessories fill the little gaps around our homes. They can warm up a sparse corner, adorn an empty table-top, or inject a little unexpected personality (as my plastic figure does). Decorative accessories can be anything. Some ideas for low-cost accessories include bowls of seashells, pottery, signs, children's artwork, wreaths—anything you love!

Screened Wall Pockets

Looking for a stylish way to stash magazines, toys, books, or other items? This budget home decorating project was designed for charm and versatility. Constructed from galvanized metal, furniture buttons, and window screening, it is easy to craft and full of decorating possibilities (see example in illustration 7-E).

You will need
Art brush
Outdoor acrylic paint for buttons
   (We used DecoArt Patio Paint in Black.)
7 1/2" furniture buttons
Pencil
Metal shears
Galvanized sheet metal (10" Handyman Coil)

Black fine-tip marker
Scissors
Aluminum window screening
Ruler (clear quilting ruler works best)
Hammer
1 finishing nail
Drill with 3/32" bit
Philips screwdriver
7 #4 by 1/2" wood screws
30" length of Picture-Mirror Cord (or 19-gauge wire)
Wire cutter

How to do it

Note: These instructions are for one 9" by 11" pocket that has a 3"-wide opening at the top. To create different sizes, follow this formula: top screen width (cut, not folded, size) = width of metal sheet + 3" and screen height (cut, not folded, size) = height of metal sheet − 1".

1. Paint furniture buttons and set aside to dry.

   Note: To seal the buttons for outdoor use, be sure to paint the back of the button.

2. Using the pencil and shears, mark and cut a 9" by 11" rectangle from the metal.

3. Using the marker and scissors, mark and cut a 12" by 10" rectangle from the screening.

4. Place the screen in front of you with the rectangle's 12" sides running horizontal.

5. Angle the sides so the top is 4" wider than the bottom. On the bottom edge, place a mark 2" in from the left corner.

6. Draw a line from this mark to the top left corner.

7. Back on the bottom edge make another mark, this one 2" in from the right corner.

8. Draw a line from this mark to the left top corner.

9. Cut the screening along these lines.

10. To fold the screening over, use a ruler to keep the edge straight. Lay a ruler along one side, $1/2$" in from the edge. As you press down firmly on the ruler with one hand, slide the other under the screening and push it up against the edge of the ruler. Work slowly, increasing the angle of the fold gradually.

11. Once the screening is folded over the ruler, remove the ruler from under the fold, place it on top of the fold, and press on the ruler to flatten the fold.

12. Repeat on the other sides.

13. Trim any rough edges flush along the folds.

14. Place a mark on the metal sheet in the bottom right-hand corner, 1" up from the bottom and $1/4$" in from the right edge.

15. Place another mark in the bottom left-hand corner, 1 inch up from the bottom and $1 1/4$" in from the left edge.

16. In the top right-hand corner, place a mark $1 5/8$" inches down and $3/4$" in.

17. Do the same in the top left-hand corner.

18. On the top corners of the screening, place a mark $1/4$" down and $1/4$" in from the edges.

19. On the bottom corners of the screening place a mark $1/4"$ up and $1/4"$ in from the edges.

20. Lay the screening on top of the metal sheet lining up the bottom marks.

21. Use the hammer and nail to punch a hole through the screening and the metal sheet on the bottom marks.

    Note: Drill bits like to slide on metal. By prepunching the hole, the bit stays in place. The drill smoothes the hole so a screw can be inserted.

22. Drill a hole through the punch.

23. Insert a screw from the back of the metal sheet and twist through the screening for a few turns.

24. Predrill a hole in the back center of the furniture buttons.

25. Place a furniture button on the screw and turn screw until tight.

26. Line up the top marks on the screening with those on the metal.

27. Punch, drill, and insert screw. Attach furniture buttons.

28. Place a mark on the left-hand side of the screen $1/4"$ in from the edge and halfway between the two furniture buttons.

29. Punch, drill, and insert screw. Attach furniture buttons.

30. Repeat on the right side and on the bottom.

31. To make the hanger for the wall pocket, wrap one end of the wire around one of the top furniture buttons by placing the last 3" of one end of the wire against the outside of a furniture button. Bring the short end around the button and wrap it around the long end of wire two times.

32. Trim off excess. Repeat on the other side.

Note: To paint the wall pockets, wipe the metal sheet clean with mineral spirits. Then use a metal primer specifically for use on galvanized metal. (Galvanized metal has an oily finish, so paint doesn't always want to adhere to it.) Next spray with a metal paint. Allow the paint to dry thoroughly before attaching the screening.

Reprinted with permission from www.wallflowers.net.

Illustration 7-E. A completed Screened Wall Pocket.

Accessories You Can Make

Accessories make your apartment look great and can go a long way by injecting personality and style into any room. But buying them can really cut into your budget, especially if you have few or no accessories already. Certainly, shopping at consignment shops, yard sales, flea markets, and discount stores can help you stay on budget. But if you'd like to save even more, you can try making some of these simple accessories:

❖ **Napkin rings.** Purchase artistic or electrical wire and string plastic or glass beads on a section that's at least 6" long. Wrap the beaded wire into a circle several times, leaving enough space to fit in a cloth napkin. Twist the lose ends into "swirls" with needle-nose pliers for a finished look.

❖ **Candlesticks.** Take wooden spindles of various sizes, and cut a round hole into the top, about 1/2" deep. Paint and decorate them and place taper candles into the opening.

❖ **Chalkboard.** Purchase plywood and trim to your desired size. Prime the surface with paint, then tape off the area you'd like to use as a chalkboard. Apply chalkboard paint, then finish the rest of the piece in the paint color of your choice. For extra interest, attach a ribbon at the top for hanging.

Accessories That Say "You"

If you don't have many accessories, you may find it somewhat overwhelming when you set out to find some that are right for your apartment. After all, there is so much to choose from. And if your budget is tight, you'll want to choose carefully and maximize the statement your accessories make in your space.

A good way to start is by selecting a theme (e.g., a hobby or interest of yours) and trying to find accessories that relate to it. You'll not only be able to spruce up your rooms but also share a little bit of yourself with everyone who visits. Here are some ideas:

- ◎ Bowler—a set of old bowling pins
- ◎ Gardener—antique tools and bowls full of seed packs
- ◎ Athlete—framed sports jerseys
- ◎ Parent—framed baby clothes (see example in illustration 7-F)
- ◎ Movie buff—old theater marquee letters
- ◎ Artist—empty frames and paintbrushes
- ◎ Tailor—a dress form and decorative thimbles
- ◎ Writer—books, pens, and an old typewriter

Illustration 7-F Parent grouping: framed baby clothes.

Great-Smelling Home Accessories

What's the first thing you notice about a home the moment you enter, before you have a chance to look around? Many people answer: the smell. Every home has a smell all its own. That smell comes from a combination of things such as the food cooked there, the cologne worn by the residents, and the products used for cleaning. As an apartment dweller, your place may even have some lin-

Easy Ways to Embellish Furniture and Accessories

You know how important your furniture and accessories are in giving your apartment personality. But sometimes your budget may not allow for some really special additions to punch up your decor.

Have you ever admired a spectacular lamp or unusual chair but sadly passed it by because it was simply too expensive? Don't feel bad—we've all been there. And just because you're strapped for decorating cash doesn't mean you can't have unique and wonderful things. In fact, picking up used or inexpensive pieces that are uncomplicated in design is great for several reasons. Not only can simply designed furnishings work well with changing styles, but they can also be embellished using inexpensive materials. Some materials that are perfect for such projects include these:

❖ **Beads.** Add glass or plastic beads to throw pillows, curtains, shades, and picture frames.

❖ **Paint markers.** For just a few dollars per color, you can add a permanent pick-me-up to tablecloths, cloth napkins, furniture, and even glass items.

❖ **Ribbon.** Trim anything from furniture to walls to bulletin boards with clearance-rack rolls of ribbon.

❖ **Plastic greenery.** Wrap plastic ivy around curtain rods, use it as tiebacks, or drape it over framed artwork for a romantic touch.

❖ **Plastic flowers.** Attach plastic flowers to anything that needs to be freshened up, such as simple curtain rods, wicker baskets, and bed canopies. For picture frames, glue small flowers around the sides for a fresh look.

gering smells, good and bad, from previous tenants. Sometimes these scents are trapped in carpeting and window treatments. But hopefully, your landlord or the previous tenant thoroughly cleaned the apartment before you moved in, so you're starting with a fresh, clean slate.

If you want to have a great-smelling home, you have many commercial products to choose from, such as carpet fresheners and air freshening sprays, candles, and solids. Many of these items are very effective in getting rid of odors and providing temporary, pleasant scents to environments. Although some of the commercial products may seem a bit too perfumy to sensitive noses, you can typically find lighter scents at discount stores and grocery stores very easily.

If you're looking for something more natural, aromatherapy items such as incense, candles, and oils might be just what you need. Aromatherapy is the ancient art of using fragrance to heal the mind, body, and spirit. Essential oils are the plant essences used in aromatherapy, and each oil has its own unique healing properties. Aromatherapy items have become quite popular over the last few years, and such items are widely available at bath shops, discount stores, boutiques, and many other retail establishments. You can also find these items priced affordably on various Web sites. (More and more crop up every day, so simply go to a search engine and search for "Aromatherapy" for listings of Web-based companies selling such items. Be sure to check the site for secure ordering technology before you buy from it.)

If you're interested in aromatherapy and looking for incense, essential oils, and candle scents with specific qualities, use the following as a guide:

- Bergamot has a citrus scent and can help relieve anxiety and depression.

- Eucalyptus has a minty, woody scent and can help clear up sinus congestion.

- Jasmine is a floral scent said to help alleviate depression and calm nerves.

- Lavender, a floral scent, is widely used for relaxation and can even help with insomnia, headaches, and congestion.

- Orange has a citrus scent that can reduce stress and lift spirits.

- Patchouli is a musty, earthy scent that is good for the skin.

- Ylang ylang is a floral scent and often used to relieve stress and promote relaxation.

Green Accessories

Accessories don't just come from stores. In fact, some of the nicest accessories come from nature. Adding these "green accessories" to your apartment can add something no inanimate object can—life. Try these simple ideas:

❖ An herb garden in a windowbox mounted inside your kitchen window

❖ Curtain tiebacks made from grapevine

❖ Topiaries—real or fake

❖ Arrangements that include fruit, leaves, and flowers

❖ Potted plants—from small enough for your windowsill to tree-size

Holiday Decorating

Everyone has a favorite holiday. For me, it's Christmas, with the smells, the twinkling lights, and the music floating through the air. One of my friends loves Easter because of the pastel colors and the fresh spring air. Plus, she really loves bunny rabbits.

When it comes to celebrating holidays, decorating your apartment in a special way can be lots of fun, particularly if the holiday will include a gathering at your place for family or friends. But I was struck in recent years by the cost of holiday decorations. On a recent Christmas shopping trip to a popular home decorating store, I was shocked at the cost of ornaments and other decorative items.

If you're the type that likes to decorate up a storm to celebrate holidays, it can be discouraging to learn that seasonal decorations can often break your bank. It's even more discouraging when you consider that these decorations are temporary, pulled out for just a few weeks a year.

Illustration 7-G. Independence Day theme: flower arrangement containing little American flags.

But then I remembered back to when I was a child, and I realized that holiday decorating was once a very simple, inexpensive undertaking. Remember when garland was something made from string, popcorn, and cranberries? And of course, coloring real eggs at Easter is a fond memory for many people, myself included.

When you approach holiday decorating, try to remember that you're doing more than decorating–you're creating a memory. While a box of expensive, crystal ornaments from a department store may be beautiful to look at, decorating plain glass with your neighbor or your niece not only results in a decorative item, it creates a warm memory that you'll recall each year as you decorate your tree.

For ideas on how to decorate on a tight budget for several different holidays, check the "'Tis the Season to Accessorize" sidebar below.

'Tis the Season to Accessorize

Remember being a kid, when you would "feel" the holidays as they approached? Our teachers would decorate the school, stores would put out new displays, and some towns would even decorate their main streets.

If you enjoy holidays throughout the year, why not do something a little special at home to reflect it? Some simple ways to get into the spirit for various holidays include these:

- **Independence Day.** Add little American flags to your existing centerpieces and flower arrangements (see example in illustration 7-G); create a new flower arrangement by placing red and white carnations in a blue vase.

- **Halloween.** Make votive holders by cutting the tops out of tiny pumpkins; make your own "ghosts" by placing a rolled-up sock in the center of a handkerchief and cinching in with a rubber band and drawing eyes on it. Hang these from clear plastic thread throughout your apartment.

- **Thanksgiving.** Create a floral arrangement with a few branches retrieved from the outdoors with autumn leaves still attached; create centerpieces of walnuts and vegetables; lay gourds and pine cones on tables as free-flowing decoration.

- **Christmas.** Wrap strands of tiny lights around your larger indoor plants; fill bowls with ornaments and set them out on your tables; cut a wreath form out of poster board and attach all your holiday cards to it; instead of ornaments, decorate your tree by tying raffia bows on the branches.

chapter 8

Get Creative
in Every Room

Every space in your apartment probably has some room for improvement, whether it be a little improvement or a lot. You've had that feeling, haven't you? That sense that the room's flow isn't quite perfect, the colors aren't right, or something is missing. Sometimes it's barely noticeable, nagging little thought that comes and goes. In other rooms, it may scream at you the moment you step inside. It all depends on your sensitivity to your surroundings and your perception of how serious the problem is. But if a room isn't working, it may be very difficult to ignore and hard to enjoy the time you spend there.

Sometimes you can attack a room's problems easily by painting the walls a different color, moving around furniture, or adding or removing accessories. You may stumble across a fix with little planning, or you may need to draw from your mental repertoire of decorating hits and misses from the past. Either way, it's a pretty wonderful feeling to triumph over a room's difficulties and end up with a comfortable, usable space.

Sometimes, how to improve a room is not at all clear. Perhaps you've lived with the room in its current state for a long time, and you just don't know where to begin to make changes. Perhaps the room is small and you have few options for making a lot of changes, particularly to the furniture layout. Or maybe you're not completely confident in your decorating abilities, and you're afraid you'll make mistakes. Well, the truth is, there are few decorating mistakes that can't be fixed. Choose the wrong paint color? Just paint over it. Position your furniture awkwardly? Roll up your sleeves and move it around again. Create a grouping that just doesn't work they way you'd hoped? No problem—take it apart and start over.

I'll share a little secret with you: I have learned much more from my decorating mistakes than I have from my successes. As a person who is intensely affected by my surroundings, I will confess that a poorly arranged bedroom once rendered me unable to sleep for weeks. And when I worked for a month in a home office with critical design errors (particularly an inefficient layout), I am certain that my productivity dropped significantly because of my constant discomfort in the space. But eventually, I identified and fixed the problems in both of these rooms, and now I can sleep and work again. So when you have a problem area, remember: You can and you will find a decorating solution. It might just take a little time.

Kitchens and Dining Rooms

They don't call kitchens "the heart of the home" for nothing. Of course, kitchens will probably always serve their original purpose—to be an area where food is stored, prepared, and (if you have enough space) consumed. But many kitchens are much more than that. Think of your last party or small get-together. Where did your friends or family members gather? Many people will quickly answer, "The kitchen." It's a place where guests feel at ease with food and drink and can easily converse with hosts who may be tied up with additional food preparations.

For families, the kitchen may be a central location where everyone's lives come together. It may be the place where children complete homework so they can be near a parent or care provider if they have questions. It may be the place where calendars, phone messages, and papers to sign for school are kept, as well as mail. For roommates and couples, the kitchen is a great place to connect and discuss everything from decorating to paying bills. Kitchens, in all their glory, are for many people the most important place in their home.

Whatever you use your kitchen for and however often you use it, it can be a beautiful and efficient space. But some of you may be wondering, "What do I need there, and how do I decorate and set up my kitchen to make the most of it?" Just start with what you need, then add from there.

Necessities

No matter what your goals in your kitchen may be, your apartment (particularly if it's a rental) likely came equipped with a stove, oven, refrigerator, and perhaps a microwave. You'll probably want to add a few more small appliances like a toaster, coffee maker, can opener, and those types of things. Once you're stocked with what you consider to be the necessary tools, it's time to get down to decorating.

If you have a small, galley-style kitchen, your space is limited and efficiency is paramount. If you have even a little space for dining, try using a small bistro set (see example in illustration 8-A). They're available at patio furniture and discount stores, as well as at flea markets. They come in wrought iron, plastic, and other materials, and many can even be

Illustration 8-A. A bistro set in the corner of a small kitchen.

Ten Decorating Web Sites You Shouldn't Miss

Before "surfing the Web" became a common phrase, locating information on budget decorating was touch and go. To find project ideas, budget decorating enthusiasts would turn to magazines, books, and some television programs. All of these were and still remain great resources. But what if you need a project idea or a question answered *now*?

The instant nature of the Internet makes it possible for anyone with an Internet connection to go online and get answers or gather ideas in minutes. But some amateur decorators can get a little overwhelmed by the sheer volume of information available to them. "Where do I even begin to find decorating resources on the Web?" many people have asked me. Many sites are available that can help you plan and organize your efforts, as well as inspire you. Here are a few of my favorites:

1. **Suite 101** (www.suite101.com). A community of more than 1,000 contributing editors who write articles and host bulletin board discussions on every topic under the sun. Suite 101's home and garden topics include budget decorating, decorating styles, kitchen design, furniture recycling, bohemian balcony (apartment balcony gardening), and many, many others.

2. **Decorator Secrets** (www.decoratorsecrets.com). Tips, projects, forums, a newsletter—this one has it all! Few sites seem to compare to this popular, well-organized grouping of decorating information.

3. **Wallflowers** (www.wallflowers.net). This site has a wonderful collection of low-budget projects with complete instructions and photos.

4. **Country Living** (www.countryliving.com). Like the print magazine that continues to set the standard for Country decorating, this Web site is packed with creative ideas and inspiration. Be sure to check out the "Community" message boards while you're there.

5. **Mikes Art** (www.mikesart.com). Billed as the Home/Garden Meta-Magazine, this site has what seems like an endless amount of information on every aspect of decorating and links to many other great sites.

6. **Living and Entertaining** (www.livingandentertaining.com). What I love most about this site: the tips and ideas are easy for even the most timid amateur decorator. Be sure to sign up for the weekly e-mails for additional tips and fun ideas for sprucing up your home.

7. **Christopher Lowell—The Official Web Site** (dsc.discovery.com/dscdaytime/christopherlowell/christopherlowell.html). There's no one quite like him, and his fans are loyal to the end. Probably because he dispenses some of the most sound decorating advice around, with his own fantastic flair. Check out his popular decorating show's Web site to find out why he's adored by millions.

8. **eHow** (www.ehow.com). The Decorating and Design (under Home and Garden) area of this huge how-to site offers step-by-step instructions on accessorizing every room in your home, choosing paint colors, and hundreds of other decorating-related topics. And many of them have a budget-conscious slant.

9. **Home and Garden Television** (www.hgtv.com). This site features guides to HGTV's television programs, instructions for decorating projects, and handy calculators to help you determine things like how much paint you need to cover a room.

10. **ivillage's Decorating Department** (www.ivillage.com /home/decorate/). Experts on everything from cleaning to bargain decorating lead the way on this energetic site that's loaded with awesome ideas.

used outdoors for summer breakfasts on the deck. They tend to seat one or two people comfortably and are very compact. (Look for the kind with chairs that tuck neatly under the table.)

Other small-scale dining options include these:

- Pairing a rolling cart/cutting board with a chair or two, and the set can fit two needs—dining and food preparation.

- Pulling barstools up to a counter (works best if there's an overhang) for informal dining at its best.

If your kitchen is larger, you'll have more dining options, but don't feel like you have to use one of the old standbys. While traditional dinette sets can be found in many retail stores, you can save money by thinking creatively. Try some of these cost-effective alternatives to purchasing new sets:

- Paint an old dinette set in a striking color, and then add special interest to the tabletop by creating a mosaic. Just break up tile, secure it onto the table, and add grout.

- Buy a small table and chairs in unfinished wood, and try a decorative painting technique instead of just staining.

- Can't afford a dinette? Find an inexpensive, fold-up card table and toss a pretty tablecloth over it. (No one will ever know the difference.) Put slipcovers on folding metal chairs to complete the set.

Beyond Necessities

If you spend a lot of time in your kitchen, you might not want to stop at just the necessities. You might want to just keep going until you've created a truly special place to serve as the heart of your home.

Decorating Tools You Should Never Be Without

As you gather decorating ideas and projects you'd like to tackle, you'll probably notice that several tools and basic necessities seem to be needed often. This is precisely why it's a good idea to hit your local discount store in search of these decoration essentials.

Some tools and accessories you may want to pick up include:

- **Hot glue gun.** This is the indispensable tool that's the crafter's equivalent of duct tape.

- **Good scissors.** Be sure to keep them sharp, and don't try to cut anything too hard since they can get damaged in the process.

- **Sheets.** Snatch up supercheap irregulars whenever you spot them. They can become shower curtains, slipcovers, tablecloths, and many other decorative items later on.

- **Baskets.** You can paint them, fill them with treasures, and put them everywhere. They're as wonderful to look at as they are useful.

- **Acrylic paints.** Hit craft stores when they're on sale, and stock up on small bottles for as little as 50 cents each. They last a long time and you'll use them eventually.

- **Paint markers.** If freehand painting intimidates you, paint markers are a great option. They provide more control than a paintbrush and come in a huge variety of colors.

- **Fabric.** Check the remnants table for big markdowns at your local fabric store. Hang on to them and eventually the perfect use will appear.

If your apartment kitchen is small, one way to start your kitchen decorating endeavors is to look up. What do you see? Consider these way-up-there ideas:

⊚ If your cabinets do not meet the ceiling, you probably have some over-the-cabinet space for displaying treasures or even for storing seldom-used items.

⊚ Hang a pot rack from your ceiling to display your cookware when it's not in use (see example in illustration 8-B).

⊚ Hang drying flowers and herbs from pegs mounted on your wall near the ceiling. (Or make this look permanent by stenciling such a scene in the same spot.)

Illustration 8-B. A pot rack holding pots and pans.

Many people with ample space in their kitchens also like to add a desk to catch bills, correspondence, and other personal papers. Although some apartments (particularly newer ones) have the luxury of a built-in desk area, you don't have to give it up if it wasn't there when you moved in. Look for small desks at yard sales, flea markets, and places like The Container Store and IKEA. You can also purchase grid systems (also available at The Container Store) for your wall and hook on little receptacles for everything from stamps to eyeglasses to mail.

If you don't have the budget for major kitchen redecorating, you can still enhance your kitchen decor easily and inexpensively. For instance, if you have a tile backsplash, you can add some beautiful tile appliqués to dress it up (they're available in a variety of colors and designs). New drawer pulls can also make a fun and interesting statement, and they're now available at crafts and home improvement stores in many different styles and colors. (If you rent, you can take them with you to your next apartment. So hang on to the original cabinet and drawer pulls so you can put them back before you move out!)

Simple Rearrangements

Unless your kitchen is fairly large, you may not have a lot of opportunity to rearrange the furnishings in it. (Particularly because many things in the kitchen can't be easily moved, such as sinks, stoves, and probably your refrigerator.) So when you're rearranging in your kitchen, you're likely to be moving small appliances, accessories, and a little furniture.

Well you're standing in your kitchen and you're ready to rearrange what you have. What can you do? Try these ideas:

Illustration 8-C A floorcloth used to enhance linoleum.

❖ **Bring out what you use.** If you use it often, why are you hiding it in a drawer or cabinet? Bring out your pots and pans and hang them from a ceiling pot rack; gather wooden spoons and display them in a Ball jar or porcelain pitcher; place your spice bottles in a pretty basket on your counter. You'll also have more space for food and china with all this cabinet cleaning!

❖ **Create a backsplash.** Tile backsplashes are wonderful, but not everyone is lucky enough to have them. But you can fashion your own creative backsplash using paint and stencils; wallpaper; inexpensive beaded board paneling; or lattice trimmed to size.

Five Creative Uses for Pottery

What can you do with a $2 clay pot? Where do I even begin? The container that was once considered suited only for holding plants has become a favorite material for budget decorators. They're inexpensive, come in variety of sizes, and are easy to find. If you're ready to try some new uses for these little gems, consider these ideas:

1. If you have children in your life, clay pots can be used for a wonderful project. Create a "Memory Pot" by lining off several vertical sections of equal width, asking the child to tell you their favorite things (e.g., color, animal, or game), and write his or her reply at the top of the section. Have the child paint pictures of these favorites with paint markers, and you'll never forget that at the age of four, your niece loved zebras, Chutes and Ladders, and the color purple.

2. Use clay pots to store your necessities in all the rooms in your apartment—writing instruments, hair accessories, paintbrushes, rolled up washcloths, and even potpourri. And since clay pots typically come with a drain hole at the bottom, they're great for holding toothbrushes and toothpaste, as they won't trap dripping water.

3. Use clay pots when entertaining. They're great for holding utensils, candy, peanuts, hostess gifts, and cloth napkins.

4. Purchase several tiny clay pots, and use them to hold votive candles.

5. Use larger clay pots as a table base or to hold collections such as dolls, rugs, and books.

❖ **Cover that linoleum.** If your kitchen floor's better days came in the last decade, you may think you're stuck. But the answer can be simple—just cover it up. Sisal rugs are casual and can be painted, and floor cloths clean up easily and can be created to the exact size you need (see example in illustration 8-C).

Bathrooms

What makes your bathroom such a special place? Maybe because it's such a private space. Most of your bathroom time is probably spent alone. Remember those "Calgon, take me away" commercials? This is how many of us grew up thinking bathrooms should be—calm, relaxing, and perhaps even providing some therapy after we'd dealt with a day out in the big, cruel world.

But when you think of decorating your apartment, you might not place your bathroom high on your list of priorities—perhaps because bathrooms tend to be the smallest room in many apartment homes, perhaps because most of us don't spend as much time there as we do in other rooms. But think of it this way: Your bathroom is where you begin and end your day. In this space, you transition from sleep to activity, then from activity to sleep again. It's where we cleanse and groom ourselves, and if you hate your bathroom, you might not be starting or ending your day off very well.

First, let's talk size. There isn't much you can do about the size of your bathroom if you rent, so it may be best to just accept the size of it and get on with decorating it. I've lived with bathrooms that are very large and bathrooms that are so tiny two people couldn't fit into them if they tried. Each type of space has its own unique challenges as well as advantages. So here's the key: Working with the layout and space you have, focus on creating a room this is efficient and attractive, and, most of all, make it a nice, happy place to be.

Necessities

Your apartment bathroom will likely come equipped with a shower and/or tub, a sink, a mirror, and some sort of cabinet, though the size, quality, and style of these items will vary.

Storage is high on many apartment dwellers' lists of bathroom necessities—particularly those with very small bathrooms, those with pedestal sinks with no storage below, and those with a wall-mounted mirror and little or no cabinet space. While pedestal sinks can be lovely and large wall-mounted mirrors come in handy for grooming, you'll still need a place for your toiletries. Some storage ideas for your bathroom necessities include the following:

- **Baskets.** Keep them in a closet or cabinet, or leave them out in plain sight—they're great either way. Fill them with towels and toiletries, and they're a stylish storage solution.

- **Over the commode.** You've probably seen these units, and they're great space savers. You can find these at discount, bed and bath, and home improvement stores.

- **Sink skirts.** Purchase or make a simple sink skirt (for pedestal sinks), and you'll earn a few feet of storage in a very convenient place.

Other necessities include bath-related items, such as a shower curtain, towel bars, and bath accessory holders. While you can certainly head down to your local bed and bath shop (or search their Web sites) for these items, you may want to consider some creative ideas:

- Use a tablecloth or flat sheet paired with a shower curtain liner for a soft, unique traditional shower curtain alternative.

❖ Hang decorative hooks instead of towel bars in your bathroom for towels, your robe, and other items.

❖ Forgo traditional shelving in favor of something more interesting. Try hanging wooden crates, rectangular baskets, and even old soda bottle crates on the wall for storing necessities and displaying accessories.

Beyond Necessities

After your necessities are in place, it's time to have some fun. Your bathroom, like your kitchen, may be full of things that really can't be moved around (your shower, your sink), so creative accessorizing will be the key to decorating your bathroom.

One visit to your local bed and bath store is probably all you'll need to realize that bath accessories come in every conceivable color, style, and theme. You can purchase completely matched sets that include everything, such as a shower curtain hooks, towels, trash cans, and a toothbrush holder. If you like a very coordinated look, these sets can be a good way to go. But I should offer you a word of caution if you're considering buying such sets: Be careful about overdoing a theme. If every last thing in your bathroom sports pink and green fishes, you may get tired of this motif after a while. If you stick with solid colors and adaptable designs, such as stripes, you may be happier with your choice for longer. You can always add splashes of other colors and themes in smaller doses with artwork and towels.

If you're not the perfectly matched-set type, you'll have many creative ways to accessorize your bathroom. Here are some creative ideas for bathroom accessories that won't break the bank:

- **Toothpaste and toothbrush holders.** Forget the plastic! Try pretty glasses, porcelain mugs, and even crystal instead.

- **Candles.** You haven't known true bath-time luxury until you're bathed by candlelight. Try lining up scented candles along the edge or your tub, and get ready for a spa-like experience.

- **Art.** Resist the urge to buy "bathroom art." (You've seen this—the little framed prints of bubble-filled tubs.) Instead choose floral prints, landscapes, or other soothing images. Art alternatives include decorative plates and wreaths.

- **Lamps.** A small lamp with a low-wattage bulb will help make late-night visits to the bathroom less jarring on sleepy eyes.

Simple Rearrangements

If your bathroom is small, your ability to rearrange things could be very limited. But rearranging can give your bathroom a little lift if it needs one.

One way to start is by opening your cabinets. What are you hiding in there, and does it need to be hidden? A glass vase on the counter can hold bars of soap and add a fresh clean smell to the room. You can also place toilet paper rolls in a pretty basket on the floor (or on a table, shelf, or vanity chair) beside the commode. (This makes it easy for guests to replace rolls without feeling like they're intruding into your cabinets.) Washcloths can also come out of the linen closet too. Just roll them up and place them in a wire basket or tin bucket, and they'll always be stylishly within reach when you need one.

Basic Feng Shui

In the 1980s, many people's lives were filled with things—cars, home, vacations, stressful jobs. Then in the 1990s, something wonderful happened to many of those same people. By middle of the decade, the insatiable desire for more and more stuff began to subside. People signed up for yoga classes, books on spirituality became best-sellers, and many former yuppies realized they needed more meaning in their lives. People began to analyze everything and try to improve their lifestyles by adding a better balance.

Not surprisingly, *feng shui* became extremely popular around the same time. Feng shui addresses the relationship between a person and his or her environment, emphasizing harmony. This ancient Chinese philosophy is said to have been around for three thousand years. Now, the masses are more than ready for it, and it has become a commonly used term.

Crucial to feng shui is the concept of ch'i. Ch'i, in Chinese culture, is an energy that's in everything you find in an environment. If you have good feng shui, your environment is kind of like a spring breeze—everything flows nicely. But sometimes ch'i gets stuck or depleted. Ch'i also enters and leaves through doors and windows (opened or closed). So in a room with awkward corners or furniture blocking your path, the ch'i is not good because there's no flow.

If you want to dabble in feng shui on a budget, here are a few low-cost ideas to get you started:

❖ **Add mirrors.** Mirrors are used widely in feng shui, and if used properly, they can help your environment immensely. Mirrors should be usable by the tallest member of the family and reflect at least six inches of clear space around your head.

❖ **Clear it out.** Is there a chair that people always seem to trip over? Are there corners that are so blocked off that they are rarely vacuumed and have layers of dust weighing them down? Move things around so the air (and people) can circulate effortlessly.

❖ **Remove clutter.** Clutter makes ch'i stagnate, so haul off your piles of junk by recycling or donating items, and your reward will be even greater.

❖ **Get even.** Don't use one candlestick or three—two or any other even number will feel better and more balanced.

❖ **Pitch it.** If it makes you sad, get rid of it. (You know, like that vase your cheating ex-boyfriend gave you or that bedspread you hate but bought because it was on sale.)

Living Rooms

If the kitchen is the heart of the home, the living room is probably a close second. Living rooms are truly wonderful inventions. Most don't serve a specific purpose, like the kitchen which is set up for cooking or a bathroom which is set up for personal care. Instead, living rooms are there for whatever you'd like to do in them—sitting around, having intense family conversations, taking Saturday afternoon naps, watching Monday night football games. Living rooms are just meant to be a place where you can "live," and what you do there is up to you.

There are no standard styles or rules that work for every living room. The furniture and accessories you can purchase for yours span every possible style and price range. Most people enjoy having a living room that reflects their lifestyle. My society-type acquaintances have lavish, richly decorated, painted, and furnished living rooms with grand pianos and fabulous artwork. Just sitting in these rooms makes me feel elegant.

Several of my friends and family members have casual living rooms that go beyond being comfortable—they are inviting. You probably have friends with living rooms like this. The rooms with huge comfy chairs, ottomans for feet propping, a television in just the right spot, fluffy throws within reach on cold evenings, and other such luxuries. These are rooms that seem to wrap their arms around you and give you a big hug that welcomes you in whenever you visit.

No matter what style of living room suits your taste, personality, and style, your living room should be a place where you feel at ease, warm, and safe.

Necessities

At a minimum, you will likely want your living room to include a sofa, a loveseat or chair, a lamp, and at least one table for setting down drinks. You also may need a place for electronic equipment such as an entertainment unit, and side tables to hold lamps and accents.

When it comes to locating living room furnishings, you'll have many options, depending on your budget. Some furniture stores (such as Rooms to Go) offer complete room sets. You can purchase single pieces or the entire room, right down to the artwork and area rugs. For people who feel they lack decorating talent (although it's probably not true), those who are too busy to shop around, and those who like finding it all in one place, such furniture stores may be a good option.

Other apartment dwellers prefer to shop around, pick and choose, and check out all their options as they put together their living rooms. For this group, I recommend trying not only furniture stores but yard sales, flea markets, outlet centers, unfinished wood furniture stores, Web sites, and discount membership warehouse stores. Remember that even your living room necessities don't have to be cookie-cutter furnishings. For instance, if you'd like something cost-effective and unique, try these out:

- ❖ **Sofas.** Instead of buying a sofa, opt for a daybed decorated to look like a sofa (with large pillows against the back). Daybeds are easy to find, can be very affordable, and when their back-rest pillows are removed, they're perfect for overnight guests.

Illustration 8-D. Benches stacked on each other to create an entertainment unit.

❖ **Tables.** Essentially, anything that has a flat surface and is about the right height can be used as a table. A trunk, a few suitcases, a stack of wooden wine boxes, an aluminum trash can with a piece of glass on top—any of these items can double as side tables and serve the same purpose with style.

❖ **Entertainment units.** Stack a couple of wide benches and you've got an inventive entertainment unit or bookshelves (see example in illustration 8-D).

Beyond Necessities

Once your necessities are covered, look around your living room and ask yourself a few questions:

1. What is the main color in the room, and is it the color that I want to dominate? If not, what color do I need to inject into this room?
2. Does the room reflect the style I was hoping to have (e.g., Country, Traditional, Contemporary)?
3. Does the room convey the mood I seek? (Is it casual and inviting? Is it elegant like my lifestyle? Is it fun and energetic?)
4. Is the room overdone or cluttered?
5. Does anything seem to be missing?

Entertaining Decor on a Budget

You're having a few friends over, and you want to add some special touches to your home, but you don't have much (if any) budget to spend. What can you do?

First, take stock. Look around your apartment and find accessories and furnishings that can either be put to another use or embellished. Dig out crafts supplies and decorating magazines for inspiration and find some ideas you like.

Second, decide what you need to do to make the gathering run smoothly. If you're having an intimate dinner party, you may want to focus on atmosphere (e.g., light some aromatic candles).

Third, get started! Decide on the projects you want to tackle, gather materials, and go for it. To help you get started, consider these low-cost decorating ideas:

- **Ambience.** Group candles together on a tray and intersperse pine cones, leaves, and other natural embellishments throughout the arrangement. (Great for December holidays.) A candle grouping on a mirror (take it off the wall and use it like a tray) can be very dazzling and dramatic. In the bathroom, place bowls of potpourri and light scented candles or leave out scented soaps, unwrapped, to freshen the room. If you're really daring, fill your bathtub halfway with water, and light floating candles in it.

- **Little touches.** Cloth napkins are an inexpensive way to create an elegant dining experience. If you don't have napkin rings, tie a pretty ribbon on each napkin, or string a few beads on wire, wrap it in a loose circle several times, then curl the ends of the wire with needle-nose pliers. For very casual affairs, create a fun set by placing plastic cutlery and a colorful paper napkin together, then tie them with a "curly" ribbon. (This is great for birthday parties.) Leave the sets in a bucket or basket so guests can help themselves.

- **Buffet touches.** If your gathering includes an informal buffet or outdoor picnic, fill metal buckets with ice to hold canned drinks with Country style. (Even if you have no yard, you can hold an outdoor picnic on a porch or deck!) For summer outdoor entertaining, line in-season fruits and vegetables along the center of the table and sprinkle about nuts, leaves, and other greenery for a free-form, table-length centerpiece.

With these questions answered, you can start to develop ideas for accessories that will take a room from basic to extraordinary. Study your answers and consider the following to determine what your living room needs:

IF YOU WANT TO ADD A PARTICULAR COLOR INTO THE ROOM: Purchase (or make) some inexpensive throw pillows, table runners, a mantel scarf, or window treatments that bring that color into the room. Varying the weight of the color (light, medium, and dark green, instead of just dark green) will help you create a less monochromatic, more interesting look.

IF YOU WANT TO INTRODUCE A PARTICULAR STYLE INTO THE ROOM: Think impact when looking for accessories. For a Native American style, start with one large print or area rug—better yet, make it your room's focal point. Then add additional accessories as your budget permits.

IF YOU WANT TO CREATE A CERTAIN MOOD IN A ROOM: Start with a paint color that complements your furnishings and helps foster that mood. For instance, bright colors can help create a fun mood, while soft pastels can help foster a calmer environment.

IF THE ROOM FEELS CLUTTERED: Try organizing the items in the room, and throw out whatever you don't need. Also be sure to leave a little breathing space between things.

IF YOU FEEL THE ROOM IS MISSING SOMETHING: Try to figure out what it is, and then determine whether it's something you already have. Also remember that you have more options and can stay on a tighter budget by thinking creatively and compromising just a little. If you feel you need a place to set drinks but don't have a coffee table, try using a wooden crate for a while, even if it's not perfect for the use. Having *something* there will help you take your time to locate the perfect table, instead of rushing out and buying one in desperation.

Simple Rearrangements

When you need change in your life, you might get a new haircut or buy new makeup. When you need change in your home, you might want to start by rearranging your living room.

For the most part, the living room is one of the easier rooms to rearrange, mainly because it tends to be one of the largest rooms and has the most movable furnishings. Unless your living room is very small, you should have at least a few options for rearranging your furniture and accessories in different ways.

If you've never tried this before, set aside a weekend afternoon. Recruit some help (if you need to move heavy pieces), and you may even want to sketch out some possible layouts on graph paper. If you're rearranging the entire room (as opposed to moving just your sofa), it's a good idea to empty the room as much as possible and begin with a clean slate.

When you're ready to begin, try this:

❖ Position furniture so that everyone who is seated can have a conversation without yelling or twisting awkwardly to face other people. If you have ample space and like to entertain, try to create "conversation nooks" so more than one conversation can take place at once.

❖ Check your paths and keep them clear. Walk through your living room from every entry way, and walk around all furniture (except those pieces against the wall) to make sure the pathways are clear and easy to maneuver.

❖ Free your furniture (some of it, anyway) by pulling it away from your walls. Try angling your sofa at an interesting position and see how it feels.

A New Life for Your Fireplace

Oh, the memories fireplaces hold! A crackling fire as the backdrop of the Christmas mornings of our youth. Roasting marshmallows with friends and family members, wondering why s'mores never turn out right. Warming your hands after a day of building snowmen and sledding.

But then it's all over and someone has to clean up those pesky, dirty ashes. If you've ever faced a fireplace full of sooty, black debris you know just what I mean. Cleaning out a fireplace can be a very messy job. And for this very reason, my own fireplace went unused for an entire winter. I wanted to use it; I just couldn't bear that thought of cleaning it out.

But fireplaces aren't just for fires anymore. If you want to avoid the mess, for instance, during a holiday party, but still want to create the ambience that fireplaces offer, you have another option. Simply arrange wood in your fireplace; then purchase about ten small, scented pillar candles. Place the candles on and around the wood and light it up for a gentle fire effect. (Tip: Line the base of your fireplace with something to catch the dripping candle wax.) If you'd like to light candles in your fireplace often, you can purchase candle holders especially made to fit into fireplaces. They're available in a variety of styles and sizes at decorating stores and even some discount stores.

In warm weather, you can arrange dried, silk, plastic, or real flowers in a basket or pot and set it inside your fireplace (see example in illustration 8-E). A potted plant or a group of potted plants, is also a great way to brighten up a room.

You can also use your fireplace area to display collections or interesting items. Think of how fabulous a grouping of pottery, African masks, or glass bottles would look in a fireplace! Remember that just because it's made to contain a fire doesn't mean you can't use it for something entirely different.

Bedrooms

Like your bathroom, your bedroom is a personal space, perhaps even a haven of refuge for you. Chances are, few people will visit your bedroom, so it doesn't have to be set up for anyone but you (or you and your partner). This fact makes your bedroom the perfect place to indulge yourself and do anything you like without the worries that may accompany decorating other rooms.

Necessities

In your bedroom, you will likely need a bed, a dresser, at least one night table, and a lamp. You might also like to have a chair, a vanity, an additional night table, and something to hold a television set.

Of all your necessary furnishings, I'd venture to say your bed is the most important piece of furniture in your bedroom. You've probably slept on a bad mattress or two in your life and experienced waking up tired and cranky and not at all ready to face the day. When you shop for mattresses, don't be shy about testing them out before you buy. If you'd like a headboard, they are abundant at flea markets and yard sales and also can be purchased new at furniture stores in many different styles, colors, and sizes. But if your budget is too tight for a premade headboard, there are several ways to create your own. You can try:

Illustration 8-E. A decorative basket of dried flowers in a fireplace.

Illustration 8-F. A quilt hanging from a rack to make a headboard.

- An old fireplace mantel
- A quilt, rug, or blanket hanging from a rack (see example in illustration 8-F)
- Doors or shutters hinged together
- Fabric stapled (on the back) to a wood or foam board cutout
- A mesh canopy hanging over the head of the bed
- A faux headboard painted on the wall directly behind the head of the bed

Beyond Necessities

Remember the main thing you do in your bedroom is rest. A bedroom that's filled with bright colors may not be conducive to rest for many people, but if you like it, then you should have it that way. The key is to find what makes you feel calm and relaxed, then use those concepts in your bedroom. For instance, if you love to be lulled to sleep by music, invest in a small radio and keep it in a spot that's easy to get to. If you have trouble sleeping, you might want to buy some aromatherapy candles you can light as you get ready for bed. You also might want to purchase thick curtains or shades to block out the morning light and increase your sleep time.

Simple Rearrangements

Your bedroom also should be a fairly easy room to rearrange, since much of what you're likely to find there is movable furnishings.

When you rearrange your bedroom, try to keep the following in mind:

❖ You'll probably need at least one end table and lamp, especially if you like to read in bed.

❖ You may want a place to set reading glasses and books within arm's reach of your bed, but it doesn't have to be a table. A small ladder, a small bookshelf, or even a wall-mounted shelf at the correct height works great, too.

❖ If you have a large closet and a dresser that's not too large, consider moving your dresser into your closet so all your clothing is together and easy to locate when you're dressing each morning. This also frees up floor space in the room.

Creative Doorways and Window Frames

So you've gotten creative in every room, and you're ready to just sit back and take it all in, eh? There are just a few more things you might want to look at before you relax and enjoy your budget-conscious handiwork. You may have forgotten a few areas that are often overlooked, and they're typically painted white or off-white. They're your doorways and window frames, and although they might not seem all that important in the decorating scheme of things, you'd be surprised at what a difference they can make when they're handled with care and creativity.

Consider these ideas for making your doorways and window molding a little bit special:

⊚ Purchase new or used corbels (decorative support brackets) and place them in the upper corners of a doorway.

- If you lack elaborate window moldings, stencil one right onto the wall around your most prominent windows.
- For larger doorways that have no door, install a curtain rod and hang draperies to create an elegant entry.
- Use colorful paints and paint markers to decorate door moldings (and the areas around them) to complement your room decor. If you're not confident in your artistic abilities, use stencils.
- Drape plastic grapevine over windows and doorways for a "bringing nature indoors" effect.

chapter **9**

Small Spaces

As a petite person, I've spent a lifetime hearing the old adage "Good things come in small packages." Somehow, though, I never quite applied that adage to my living space. Have we become accustomed to thinking that more is better? Perhaps, until you realize that living in small spaces does have many merits.

For instance, how much time does it take you to clean a large apartment? Now, if you lived in a smaller place, how long might it take you? Do you think you could save one, perhaps two, or even three hours a week? But cutting your cleaning time isn't the only benefit to having a small apartment. You could also think of a small space as an inspiration to edit your collections, rid yourself of clutter, and fight off the urge to be a packrat. If you don't have the space for things, letting them go is just a little easier. Plus, as a budget decorator, it's logical to surmise that small spaces require fewer furnishings and accessories, thereby enabling you to make the most of a limited decorating budget.

Even with all the practical benefits aside, small spaces can be fun, cozy, and intimate. But often, they require some creative decorating. For instance, in a small apartment, you may have fewer options for positioning furniture than you would have in larger spaces. Some rooms—such as tiny kitchens—may have no space for dining. Small spaces also pose other interesting (yet conquerable) challenges, such as finding ways to maximize storage space.

So if you're facing the task of decorating a small apartment, whether it be a flat, a townhouse, a condo, or other type of space, remember one key word that should underlie all your efforts: *function*. When your space is limited, every inch counts. If you decorate with the goal that you'll be able to accomplish whatever you need to in each room, your small space will be a fabulous place to live.

One-Room Living

We all know that apartments come in a wide variety of shapes, sizes, and layouts. Still, many of us have always believed that apartments and houses are a grouping of clear-cut, separate rooms, each designed for specific functions, and that four walls and a door designate those areas. And often, this is how it works. But not always.

As a teenager, I visited a loft apartment for the first time. It was an incredible space in an old warehouse building, situated in the ultrahip Soho section of New York City. The ceiling was soaring, and I could only guess that it was at least twenty feet high. In its original state, the loft was one, huge square with no interior walls defining any of the areas, not even the bathroom. (That was simply a commode and a shower in one corner.)

The woman who lived there was an artist, and she was quite ingenious when it came to designing, decorating, and manipulating her space. To preserve the open, airy quality of the loft but still construct some private areas, she created "walls" that were about five feet tall. They resembled office cubicle walls but were much more stylish. (Some were actually frosted glass panels that let in the light but obscured the view.) They also had wheels so she could move them around however she pleased. Using these portable walls, she created a bedroom for herself, another for her roommate, and a bathroom they shared. Her living room, kitchen, and dining room were still one large area, but she used furnishings to visually "separate" them from each other. This apartment made quite an impression on me, and I still recall it vividly, although nearly twenty years have now passed.

But lofts, popular as they are, are certainly not the only kind of one-room living available to apartment renters. Of course, tiny, plain college dorms rooms come to mind, but one-room living also includes basement apartments, apartments over garages, studio apartments, and other types of spaces.

If you're faced with the task of decorating a one-room living space, you may need to be even more creative than apartment dwellers living in more traditional spaces with clear-cut room boundaries. But don't let that scare you. One-room apartments can be wonderful places to live.

College Dorm Rooms

College dorm rooms are not typically the most glamorous places to live. But most are perfectly inhabitable, despite appearances. Dorm rooms vary in size, layout, and every other feature, but they do have something in common: they are the temporary home for college students who have busy lives and tight budgets for everything, including their decorating. In fact, decorating may not be very high on the list of priorities when you're packing up and heading to college. But remember, this place may not look like a "home," but it will be your home for at least nine months of the year. Understanding that your surroundings have a great impact on other facets of your life, you'll want to make some effort to arrange and decorate your dorm room with care.

My own college dorm room was pretty awful-looking when I first saw it. It featured a cold, industrial-looking floor, narrow bunk beds with very thin, springy mattresses, an odd loft unit, two small desks, and one large window covered with yellowing blinds. Others are set up more like apartments, with a kitchen, a living room, a bathroom, and a bedroom (or more). But no matter the layout or the size, the accommodations are rarely lavish.

If you, a family member, or a friend are off to college and don't quite know where to begin to decorate a dorm room, consider the following advice:

⊚ **Coordinate with roommates.** Touch base with your roommates to coordinate a color scheme. The idea isn't to make everything match, but to select a common color or theme (or select some color combinations) to tie things together and make the space seem more homey and less thrown together.

⊚ **Perk it up with paint.** If your college allows it, painting your room (or just one accent wall) is a great way to make it more personal and appealing. If you're willing, you can also try textures (with mitts, sponges, and other tools) or stenciling. Paint is inexpensive and easy to work with, so even if you've never painted a room in your life, you can probably handle painting your dorm room without a hitch. (Just be sure to tape off molding and use drop cloths.) Paint is also great for covering up wear and tear on worn-but-usable furniture.

⊚ **Treat your windows.** Many dorm rooms come equipped with blinds or shades, but adding a valance, swag, or full curtain can create a much cozier feel. You can make your own curtains on the cheap by purchasing sheets and cutting open the top seams so you can insert a curtain rod.

⊚ **Get artsy.** Dorm room art doesn't just mean posters of your favorite rock band, although if you want this in

your room, by all means, go for it. Framing family photos and hanging them together creates a wonderful
grouping and can help you on days when you feel a little
homesick. Also don't forget about postcards—they're
cheap, they can be framed, and some of them are wonderfully artistic. Can't afford frames? Try making your
own by cutting corrugated cardboard or heavy poster
board into a square, snipping out a hole for the photo,
and leaving an inch or two border around the photo.
Clip the photo to the frame using a binder clip, and
you've got a modern, sleek frame that makes changing
the featured art or photo a snap.

⊚ **Yard-sale it.** Visit yard sales for items like mirrors,
framed prints, shelves, and other decorative touches.
Another trick: Find secondhand art books at a low cost,
cut pictures out, and frame them.

⊚ **Break the rules.** Dorm rooms don't have things like
wrought iron dinette sets, antique rocking chairs, or
stacks of handmade quilts, do they? Sure they do—I've
seen *all* of these items in some wonderfully decorated
dorm rooms. These clever dorm dwellers broke the rules
and added things they loved to their space, rejecting the
notion that such items don't belong in college dorm
rooms. You can do it, too.

⊚ **Lighten up.** Many dorm rooms have harsh, fluorescent
lighting. This can be great for cleaning and studying,
when bright light is important. But adding a lamp or two
will help you keep the room and the mood a bit softer
when you want to.

Don't Leave for College Without These

No, you can't take it all with you. You might need to leave behind your Precious Moments figurines, all your trophies and blue ribbons, and your Beanie Baby collection. (Take a few, if you'd like, but leave the rest of your collection at home.) Remember these words as you (or your friend or family member) pack up to head for a college dorm: *be selective.* This goes for personal items as well as decorative items. Take your time, and really consider the choices your make. If you absolutely love your stuffed animals and can't get to sleep at night without them, take them with you. But realize that this probably means something else will have to stay behind.

Begin at least a few weeks before your move by creating a list of everything you think you'll need in your dorm room. Don't forget to add these decorating must-haves:

❖ **Bulletin boards and thumbtacks.** When it comes to bulletin boards, go for a large one where you can tack on everything from bills to be paid to favorite snapshots.

❖ **Pictures of family and friends.** You may be an adult, but you'll still come down with the flu or have a bad day now and then. Hanging up pictures of the people you love will help you cope through rough times.

❖ **Lounging/reading pillow and clip-on lamp.** If you purchase only two items before you leave, it should be these. Lounging pillows are more solid and heavier than pillows designed for sleeping, they have arms that enable them to sit up by themselves, and they keep you propped up nicely while you read in bed. (Some even have pockets on the arms for pens, eyeglasses, and other items.) Attach the clip-on lamp to your headboard or other convenient location, and you can easily study in bed whenever you need to.

❖ **Hanging aids.** You'll be hanging lots of things on your walls, yet these items are the easiest to forget. Don't be stuck with just thumbtacks (for your hanging) and a high-heeled shoe (for your hammering). Bring a hammer, double-sided tape, a screwdriver, small nails, screw-in hooks, nails, screws, and wall hooks that adhere with removable adhesive.

Studio Apartments

A young woman named Karen once lived in one of the tiniest studio apartments I have ever seen. I visited her shortly after she moved in, and she said, "Here, let me give you the tour." She then moved her arm outward, as if to present the room we were standing in. I planned to follow her on the rest of this "tour," but she didn't *go* anywhere. "Well, this is it," she said.

The entire apartment was the approximate size of a typical living room, and the only separate, private area (with its own walls and a door) was a bathroom. The living room and bedroom were one connected area, and the kitchen (in this case, actually a "kitchenette") consisted of a few appliances against the left-hand wall. As adorable as this diminutive, Miami Beach studio apartment was, I found myself wondering how in the world she would be able to live in the space comfortably. But she did, for more than a year. And the key seemed to be that Karen was quite good at avoiding clutter and defining functional areas, no matter how small each of those areas turned out to be.

To begin, Karen added two room-dividing screens to separate her living room and her bedroom. They were simple, Oriental-style screens (made of paper and wood) that she'd picked up for a very reasonable price. She treated the screens as if they were a wall, placing her television set in front of them, with a sofa, small coffee table, and chair positioned directly across from it. Next, she placed a very narrow cutting board cart a few feet away from the appliances and placed a high stool beside it. This created a "barrier" between the living room and the kitchenette and let people know that "the kitchen area begins here." She kept another high stool in the closet, so if she had a dinner guest, she could pull it up to the cutting board as well and create a small table for dining. And since the cutting board was on wheels, she could move it around to find the best location for dining.

Lastly, she purchased a few area rugs of varying sizes and colors, but in a similar style, and used them to define spaces. One went in the living room under the coffee table, the other in the bedroom in front of her bed, and a small one in the kitchen under the cutting board (which also kept it from rolling around when the cutting board was in use).

There was no way for Karen to hide the fact that her apartment was very, very small. But luckily, she didn't feel the need to hide it. Instead, she simply made it remarkably efficient and charming. Rather than apologize for her lack of space, she reveled in it, and today she says that some of the happiest days of her life were spent there in that pint-size space where I once wondered how she'd ever get along.

If you have a studio apartment to decorate, try some of these ideas:

- **Dividers.** Buy them or make your own from doors, shutters, even pieces of lattice. You can also separate areas with curtains. Sheers are especially nice, because they allow the light to filter through but give different areas some definition.

- **Color.** If possible, use paint to identify specific areas in a studio apartment. (For instance, you could paint one wall in each area a complementing but different color.) Also keep in mind that light colors can help a room seem larger and more open.

- **Furniture.** Resist the temptation to have only Lilliputian-sized furniture. Having a few large pieces works just fine in small spaces and may call less attention to the room's size than a collection of smaller pieces would.

Basement Apartments

Let's say you're a newlywed and saving up for a down payment on your first house. Or maybe you recently retired and just didn't need a large house anymore. Perhaps you're a live-in nanny or elder care provider, and an apartment comes with the job. There are many life and work situations that make living in a basement apartment a great option, particularly if your basement apartment comes equipped with a kitchen, bathroom, and private entrance. Some basement apartment dwellers rent from family or friends; others have a more traditional, renter/landlord setup.

If your apartment is in the basement of a house, you can create a homey place for yourself in many ways:

❖ **Create a "foyer."** Many basement apartments lack an entrance area because the basement is built to be just another room. Create a faux foyer by placing some of the following items near the door: a runner-type rug, a chair, a mirror, and a coat rack.

❖ **Warm it up.** Some basements are a little dark or cold, but you can warm it up by painting the walls with warm, rich colors.

❖ **Lighting.** If you have a drop tile ceiling in your basement apartment, you might have tube lighting built right into the ceiling. Although this may be practical, it can feel a little cold and institutional. Inject some lighting ambience with lamps, especially those with dimmers.

Multipurpose Furnishings

Let's say you work at home, even just a day or two a week. You have a lovely but compact apartment and need a place to work, so you should purchase a desk, right? No, you might not need a desk at all. Because when you have very limited space, things like desks might not fit the bill well enough. Perhaps what you really need is a dining room table that doubles as a desk until you're throwing a dinner party. Then it becomes a table again.

Let's try it again. You live in New York City and you have several friends who love to come visit you. You'd better head out and find a guest bed, right? No, perhaps you shouldn't. After all, where will you put it? Finding a couch or futon that converts into a bed would be a much wiser choice. After all, your friends don't live with you; they just come to visit every now and then.

You get the picture now. When you have limited space, you need furnishings that have multiple personalities. With some pieces, such as futons, their multipurpose nature is obvious and perhaps it's even the selling point. But as a wise and creative decorator, you will be able to find other uses for items that seem only suited for one use. You will be able to do this with practice. Some furnishings ideally suited for multiple uses include these:

- Trunks—can serve as tables as well as storage

- Benches—work as tables and extra seating

- Ottomans—a great place to prop up tired feet, but add a tray and they can double as a coffee table. They can also function as extra seating.

- Rolling cart/cutting board table—a great place to chop your vegetables, then wipe it off, throw a tablecloth over it and pull up a stool or two for casual dining. They can also be used as buffet and serving tables for dinner parties.

Split Personality Test

If you live in a small space, you know it's important to get the most out of every inch of your apartment. Furnishings and accessories with "split personalities" can help. (These are items that serve more than one purpose.) So, how do you spot such items, many of which you may already have in your home? It's easy: Just look at the things you have in your home and visualize as many additional, creative uses for them as you can. For practice, try taking this short quiz. Just match the furnishing on the left to a potential use on the right.

Furnishing/Accessory	Potential Use
1. Large copper fish poacher	A. Home office desk
2. Large wooden salad bowl	B. Sparkly candle holders
3. Narrow sofa table	C. Spice bottle and cooking oils storage
4. Rarely-used dining room table	D. Potpourri holder
5. Crystal drinking glasses	E. Buffet serving area for dinner parties

Answers: 1 = C, 2 = D, 3 = E, 4 = A, 5 = B

Movable Furnishings

Recently I went on a candle-shopping spree and came home with about seven vanilla-scented candles ranging in size from small to very large. I wanted to create a dramatic grouping with them on the coffee table in my living room, so I could light the aromatic bunch when I am entertaining. There is just one problem: my friends' kids.

Don't get me wrong, I *love* kids. (Really—I even have a couple of them myself.) But while my children are old enough to determine that candle flames are hot and that they should stay away from them, many of my friends have younger children who don't know this lesson just yet. (And I don't want them to learn it at my home!) I wanted this grouping, but I dreaded the thought of moving each and every candle when I have little visitors.

Then the answer came to me, in the form of a slightly rusted, adorable old tole tray. I have a small but growing collection of these trays, and I could never seem to find the perfect home for this one. It was a little too wide for my window sills, where I display other trays, and though I had tried other spots for it, nothing seemed right. So I placed the tray on my coffee table, arranged the candles and added a few accents—a couple of gold, star-shaped ornaments to give the arrangement additional sparkle. Placing the arrangement on this tray enabled me to move this rather heavy grouping with ease. I just grab the handles and swoop it over to the dining room or other out-of-toddler-reach location. The decorating dilemma was solved economically and easily, thanks to an accessory that is made for easy moving.

Illustration 9-A. A wagon filled with plants for balcony decoration.

Whatever the reason you may need to move things around now and then, there are many ways to do it. Some items are movable when you purchase them, and they're great to have around for a variety of uses. For instance, consider old-fashioned wagons. (They're not just for kids!) Wagons are great for potted herb gardens (roll it inside or out to your balcony, depending on the weather), toys, books, and anything that needs to move from room to room now and then (see example in illustration 9-A).

Other furnishings can be made movable by using some helpers, such as the following:

- ❖ **Furniture sliders.** I first saw these on a television home shopping channel, but now they're widely available. Slip these under furniture of any size, and moving anything is a lot easier.

- ❖ **Wheels.** Tables, chairs, benches, room dividers—just about anything can have wheels attached to it, making it a movable, usable piece.

Still other furnishings are movable because they can be easily picked up and relocated so the space they occupy can be put to other uses. Baskets are the perfect example. If your home office desk doubles as a dining room table when friends come for dinner, keep your files and other supplies in baskets instead of in stacks on your desk. When it's time to dine, just grab the baskets and stash them away.

Your Balcony as Living Space

Where does your apartment space end? At your back wall, or maybe at your back door? If you have a balcony or deck, that should be your answer. It may not look like the rest of your apartment, but don't sell it short.

"Why should I decorate my balcony? I'll just put some patio furniture out there and forget about it." I hear apartment dwellers say this often, and I usually tell them they're missing out on valuable living space. Your balcony is just as much yours as any other room in your apartment. It's just different, and it requires a different approach when it comes it decorating.

Balconies can also be very revealing too. Have you ever seen a balcony that's brimming with tons of plants and flowers? Chances are there's a nature lover or gardener working magic there. How about balconies with lots of toys on them? That's where a parent treats little ones to playtime in the sunshine. And whether that balcony is in the heart of New Orleans or the suburbs of Los Angeles or anywhere in between, you know it's the apartment dweller's instant access to fresh air any time they choose.

Keeping It Private

Some outdoor living spaces lack something that's important to most of us–privacy. It may be difficult for you to kick up your feet and settle in for a good read with a cup of hot tea when you know your neighbor is on his balcony in plain view, grilling hamburgers. Since balconies are at least partially exposed to the outside world, privacy may seem difficult (even impossible) to obtain there. But it isn't. If you have some sort of roof over your balcony or deck, try these ideas (they're great for front porches, too):

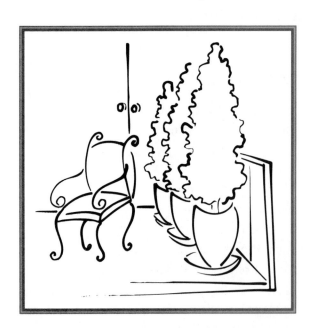

Illustration 9-B. Tall plants lined up to provide privacy on a balcony.

◉ Create a visual barrier by purchasing a weather-resistant roller shade, such as the plastic ones available at home improvement stores. Suspend the shade from the roof and each side of the balcony, and you'll block out at least some of the world. You can roll up your shades when you're ready to let the world back in.

◉ A length of heavy canvas or other water-resistant material can be hung the same way as shades and tied back like curtains when you want to invite in sun or moonlight.

◉ Line up tall, potted plants or trees on the sides of your balcony for a more natural barrier (see example in illustration 9-B).

◉ Place metal (or other weather-resistant) shelving on your balcony, and fill it with smaller plants, flowers, and even accessories such as birdhouses.

Ideas, Tips, and Tricks

❖ Need a change in your apartment? Buy new or recover your existing throw pillows. You can also dye or embellish your curtains for a boost.

❖ If you live in a basement apartment that smells a little musty (as many basements do), keep lots of great-smelling, decorative accessories around. Scented candles, bowls of potpourri, and incense are all great choices.

chapter 10

Special-Purpose Spaces

In your apartment, you probably have two types of spaces to decorate: your "predetermined spaces" and your "free spaces." Your predetermined spaces (or entire rooms, in some cases) are those that you know you need, you know exactly how you'll use them, and you know what type of furnishings you need for them. In your bedroom, for instance, you know you'll need a bed and something that stores clothing, such as a dresser. In your living room, you'll need some sort of seating, such as a sofa.

Free spaces don't fall neatly into place as predetermined spaces do. In fact, some free spaces come about almost by accident. Let's say you've just moved into an apartment, you've set up all your furnishings, and you realize you have a little more space than you thought or that you could shift your belongings a bit and end up with open areas that could be put to use. (This happened to me once. My roommate and I decided to use a small sunroom as our dining area, and we were left with a dining room that was completely unused and empty.) These areas can also be as compact as a corner of a room or even an unused closet or as large as an entire room.

A wonderful way to get the most out of a "free area" is to dedicate it to a favorite interest or hobby. Some popular hobbies that could benefit from such a space include these:

❖ **Artwork.** If you're an artist, setting up a studio area—even if it's a small, cozy one—can help foster your creativity. (Areas without carpeting work well in case of spills, or you can cover flooring before tackling messy projects.) An art table, some shelving, and ample space for storing supplies will likely be needed (see example in illustration 10-A).

Illustration 10-A. An artist's space in the corner of a living room.

❖ **Sewing.** Sewing supplies can take up lots of space, unless you plan carefully. Setting up a sewing machine on a table is a must. To keep fabric neatly stored, fold pieces then stack them neatly on book shelves, or tag baskets (e.g., by color or fabric type) and either hang them on a wall or line them up on a table or the floor. Other supplies can be accommodated by using wall grids.

❖ **Reading and writing.** Whether you're writing the great American novel or just want to read it, you can create a cozy corner with a desk, a lamp (or two), a bookshelf stuffed with great reads and reference materials, and a warm fleece blanket so you can get comfy when you read.

❖ **Computer work.** Computer desks and workstations come in every size, shape, and color you can imagine. Look for them used at flea markets and yard sales, or hit an office supply store if you're looking for a larger selection. (At least a few should be reasonably priced.) Also opt for an adjustable chair with appropriate back support, ample lighting, a printer stand, and a filing cabinet if you need to store files.

Children's Rooms and Nurseries

If you're decorating a room for a child who lives with you or visits often, you may feel like you're facing the ultimate challenge—but it can be done with style and on a budget, I assure you!

To start, consider the age of the child (or children) who will use the room and carefully ponder their needs, likes, and dislikes. The best advice I've heard on setting up a kid's room (or any rooms they'll use often) came from a Montessori school teacher. She said, "Imagine living for one day as a child in an adult world." She encourages people who live with children to study the environments they create and decide whether any obstacles can be removed to make it easier on little ones.

Some obstacles are easy to spot if you just look for them. For instance, when my son was just three years old, I found that his bathroom wasn't set up very well. Although he believed himself to be "a big boy," he was merely a toddler, and I realized that he did not have a stool in his bathroom to facilitate easier personal grooming, such as teeth brushing. An inexpensive wood stool was the answer, and he was never again forced to stand on the tips of his toes to brush his teeth or turn on the faucet. With the goal of creating a child-friendly environment in mind, I studied the environment, and spotting the absence of a stool was pretty easy.

Other obstacles are not as obvious. When my daughter was born, I placed a tall, wicker shelf unit in her room to store stuffed animals. It was inexpensive and attractive, and it did the job well for a few years. Then, we had a little mishap. At three, when my precocious toddler wanted a stuffed animal I'd placed on the top shelf, she pulled a small chair over and stood on it to reach. But when she pulled the toy, she got more than she bargained for; the entire shelf unit came tumbling down on top of her. (It must have been quite a pull!) She laughed hysterically at the shower of cascading stuffed animals and simply pushed the very light shelf unit off of her and continued to play. I, however, realized that while she had not been hurt, I hadn't really thought out the setup of her room as well as I should have. In addition, I'd made a very common mistake—I did not refine the room as she got older and her needs changed.

The solution to the tall wicker shelf unit dilemma was simple: I needed to put her stuffed animals (and other toys) within her reach, or she could never really master her own space. I swapped the tall wicker unit with a more sturdy, much shorter unit that I had in another room. I also placed an inexpensive toy hammock within her reach so she could put her animals away easily. Not only was my daughter able to reach her toys effortlessly after this minor redecorating, but she was able to put her toys away without help, and that also helped her learn more responsibility.

I continued analyzing her needs and making changes to her room by carefully observing her in the space. After a few weeks, I identified areas that needed improvement and tackled them all. Her room was much better suited to her needs, and she and I were much happier with the space as a result.

Creative Furnishings for Kids

Okay, you have to create a comfortable, safe, functional, and great-looking room for a child. You have many choices and much work to do!

First, consider furniture. If you're going the traditional, new furniture route, check out local furniture stores, especially those specializing in children's furniture. Also be sure to check the Internet for furniture, but don't forget to factor in shipping charges when you're working on your budget. (These could be considerable, depending on the size and weight of the items and the company you're purchasing them from.) Web sites are an especially great place to locate specialty items, such as hand-painted furniture.

If your budget is very limited, try consignment shops, flea markets, and yard sales first. Also check with friends, family members, and anyone else you know who may have items they are ready to part with. A word of caution: Always be very careful when purchasing used furniture for children, particularly cribs and other baby items. Such items may not meet current safety standards and should be passed up, no matter how great a bargain they may be.

If you're picturing something a bit more inventive for your kid's room, here are some ideas you might try:

- ⊚ **Beds.** If you love Country, place the head of the bed against a wall, hang a quilt behind it, and you won't even need a headboard. Iron gates, curtains, and gathering netting suspended from your ceiling can also work nicely and create one-of-a-kind bedding any kid will love.

- ⊚ **Window treatments.** Be careful when purchasing window treatments for kids' rooms, especially blinds with pull cords. (Read packaging carefully, and keep cords out of children's reach.) Curtains for children's rooms are easy to whip up with clearance sale flat sheets, acrylic paints, rubber stamps, and stencils. You can also use thermal fleece blankets (or a few yards of fleece fabric), fold over the top, and stitch it closed (leave openings for the rod), then hang it up to create a warm, casual atmosphere. Too boring? You can add interest with funky tie backs in contrasting colors, appliqués, and even by sewing on colorful buttons or pom-poms. (These small items can pose potential choking hazards for small children, so keep these embellishments out of their reach or save this idea for older kids.)

⊚ **Containers.** Long, skinny toys and sports equipment, such as baseball bats, swords, and golf clubs can pose a storage challenge. Here's a simple solution: Try an umbrella stand (available at discount stores). Long items tucked into these containers won't fall over and end up on the floor like they would with shorter containers and toy boxes, and you won't have these items lying horizontally in a closet taking up a lot of floor space.

Illustration 10-B. A reading corner.

⊚ **Cling-ons.** Several companies offer wall decorations that stick (like wallpaper) or cling on (with static) to walls. Some even come in complete theme kits. Visit decorating, paint, and home improvement stores, as well as Web sites that sell wallpaper and other decorating elements to locate these clever wall decor items.

⊚ **Artwork.** A child's room is the perfect place to display artwork created by children. Another inexpensive art solution for children's rooms is to cut artwork from storybooks, frame them, and create dramatic groupings. (Check your local used bookstore for beautifully illustrated volumes at low prices.)

⊚ **Size them up.** Attach a yardstick or two to the wall with small nails or even Velcro, and you'll have fun

seeing how quickly your little one grows. Dress up
the sticks with paint, ribbon, buttons, and other
embellishments.

⊚ **Reading corner.** Team a couple of bean bag chairs, a
small homemade bookshelf, an inexpensive area rug, and a
collection of great books, and you have a cozy corner for
reading and quiet play (see example in illustration 10-B).

⊚ **Hang-ups.** Peg boards, shelving with pegs, or even just
fanciful hooks in low places are great inspiration for kids
to hang up caps, dress-up clothes, and accessories.

Fun Themes for Kids' Bedrooms

I've seen some fabulous kids' rooms over the past ten years, as many
of my friends and associates have had children and decided to decorate wonderful rooms for them. I've seen magical castles, incredible murals, and just about every theme I can think of, tackled in
many different ways. And I must admit, I'm a sucker for a child that
grabs my hand when I enter their home and insists, "You have to
come see my room!" These kids are so comfortable in their space
and so proud of it that they want everyone they know to come see
and enjoy it too. What a wonderful compliment to the adult who
put it all together!

If you're looking for a fun kid's room theme and ideas for how
to pull it off, consider these:

❖ **Circus.** Drape your walls (or one wall, or a window) in
strips of red and white fabric (sewn together) to create a
Big Top feel. Hang a few small swings from the ceiling
with animals perched on them to simulate trapeze artists.
And a wire stretched across the room with a doll balanc-
ing on it (hang her from the ceiling with fishing line and

secure her feet the wire) gives a "walking the tightrope" feature to the room.

❖ **Nautical.** Salvage an old canoe (make sure to take safety measures, like sanding rough spots), and use it to store toys, or insert pieces of wood and create a shelf unit with it. Also hang oars, life floats, and buoys on the walls. Create a valance of nautical flags lined up and sewn together with the points facing down. (You can make your own nautical flags from sheets of felt!)

❖ **Western.** Decorate walls with wallpaper that looks like the inside of a log cabin. Pick up old cowboy boots at flea markets (any size—adults or kids) and use them to create lamps, hold potted plants, or just place them on a high wall shelf as decoration. Also display a lasso on the wall, and use cow-print fabric to create window treatments. (Be careful with long ropes around young children.)

❖ **Garden.** Use picket fencing for a headboard; a place to hold jewelry, purses, and accessories; or as decoration by just leaning up against the wall. Books and toys can be stored in oversized terra cotta (or terra cotta–like plastic) pots, and kid-sized plastic Adirondack chairs can serve as seating. Other low-budget, garden-inspired accessories include floral-patterned wallpaper borders; watering cans; sap buckets; floral design stencils; and, of course, silk and plastic flowers!

Guest Rooms

Do you, even periodically, have overnight guests? When you do, where do they sleep and keep their belongings? Do you give up your bedroom to them to assure that they are comfortable? Or, per-

A New Life for Coat Racks and Umbrella Stands

Umbrella stands and coat racks (also known coat stands and hat racks) are items many of us do without. Instead, we hang raincoats and winter jackets in closets and prop up umbrellas in out-of-the-way corners. Many people pay little or no attention to the storage of these items that we all need to have but don't really need to worry about very much.

But there are more fashionable ways to store jackets and umbrellas, and these ways can also be very affordable. Coat racks, for instance, come in a plethora of sizes, styles, and shapes, made from a variety of different materials. (Wooden coat racks are abundant at many flea markets. And they look great white-washed, for a Cottage look.) Umbrella stands also come in many different styles, and discount stores are a great place to start shopping for them.

If you still think you'd be happier stashing coats and umbrellas in a closet, don't discount umbrella stands and coat racks just yet. Although these accessories may seem to have only one use, they're actually quite versatile pieces that can be put to many creative uses.

In addition to its conventional job of holding umbrellas, an umbrella stand can be used to:

- Store baseball bats, golf clubs, and other sports equipment neatly and compactly
- Display a dried or silk flower arrangement
- Hold fire wood or kindling
- Hold an aromatic display, such as potpourri or scented pine cones

Instead of serving as a place where jackets and hats hang out, try using your coat rack for these purposes:

- Display your favorite mementos. Frame photos and artwork, secure a ribbon at the top of the frames, and hang from the arms
- Accommodate towels, robes, and toiletry holders in your bathroom
- Store purses, scarves, and other accessories in your bedroom

haps, do they simply crash on a couch or sofa sleeper and place their belongings any place they can find?

Having a guest room can be a luxury. But if you're lucky enough to have the space for one, why not do it up right? Your guests deserve it, and you can create a comfortable guest room easily and affordably. Begin by jotting down some ideas for your guest room, using your responses to the following questions as your guide:

1. What kind of atmosphere do I want to create in my guest room? (Calming and restful? Fun and exciting?)
2. What furniture is essential to this room (e.g., a bed, dresser, night table)?
3. Do I already have furnishings and accessories that I could use?
4. Is there anything I need to purchase to complete the space?

Once your wishes for the room are clear, empty out the room, if it isn't already. Paint, if that's part of your plan, and take care of any flooring needs, such as laying down an area rug. Bring in the furniture you already own or have purchased, then take a step back. Before you begin accessorizing, go back to your answers to those questions, and contemplate the mood you're going for. Your accessories are the items that will help you meet your goals and establish the mood, so choose them carefully.

For instance, if you're hoping to create a tranquil, relaxing mood, try some of these simple, low-cost ideas:

⊚ Purchase clearance rack fabric in soft tones like light blue and soft pink, and re-cover throw pillows instead of purchasing new ones.

⊚ Gather accessories according to color, and display them in new ways. For instance, if you're going for an all-white color palette, gather up all the books you have with white covers and stack them on the night stand.

⊚ Add calming touches such as scented candles, a light with a dimmer bulb, and soft fluffy pillows.

Home Offices

Eleven years ago, I set up my first home office, and many of my friends and family members were a little puzzled. "What will you do in there?" they asked, seemingly confused as to why I'd need a whole room instead of just a corner table where I could pay bills and store mail. I explained to them that I would be telecommuting, and they didn't quite get it. It was 1989, the term was little known in the business world, and people's reactions to it ranged from confused to suspect over the whole notion of combining home and work space.

Within a few years, all this changed. Most people learned more and more about telecommuting and home-based businesses, until it was accepted as a legitimate (and for many people, a preferable) way to work. Now, more than a decade after I set up my first home office, most people I know also have a fully equipped workspace in their homes, whether they work at home or not.

Today, people set up home offices for a variety of purposes, and many find that decorating these rooms can pose unique challenges. For instance, are there affordable yet attractive ways to contain inherently unattractive things like office supplies and files? And what kind of desk do you really need?

To begin decorating (or redecorating) your home office, think through some of the basics concepts important to this (and every) space:

❖ **Location.** Will you need an entire room or just a portion of a room? For the heavy use home office, an entire room (if you have one to spare) may be warranted. Or you may want to create a combination home office/guest room using a spare bedroom. Also consider the type of space you'd like to work in. If you crave natural light and views of the outdoors, try to select an area where you'll have easy access to a window. Also make sure you're near electrical outlets and a phone jack, so you won't have long cords running all over the place.

✣ **Furnishings.** A desk and chair will likely be at the top of your list of furniture needs. You may also need a filing cabinet, a printer stand, and bookshelves. Go for double-duty furnishings if your space is small. For instance, forgo a printer stand and place your printer on top of a short filing cabinet or on your bookshelf.

✣ **Lighting.** Proper lighting is crucial to every work environment. You'll likely need overhead lighting (a fixture on the ceiling that throws bright light over the entire space) and task lighting (a lamp on your desk, e.g., to simplify reading).

✣ **Accessories.** This may be a workspace, but don't forget: it's in your home, so you can decorate it in any way you please. Forget traditional office accessories like boring, Lucite desk clocks and bland art. Accessorize your home office with things that you love, whether that means framed Picasso prints, a collection of Cabbage Patch dolls, or sports memorabilia.

✣ **Walls.** I must admit there's one thing I miss about my old cubicle days in a downtown Atlanta office building: being able to pin memos and other papers to the walls. But there's an easy way to get some pin-up real estate on your home office walls: Cover a large bulletin board with fabric for a less institutional and very usable wall hanging. You can also trim the board with ribbon, fringe, or anything else that goes with your decor. Surrounding a plain chalkboard with a decorative frame is also a great way to create another productivity-boosting wall accessory. (See examples in illustration 10-C.) Also don't forget to adorn your walls with favorite photographs, artwork, or collections to create a happy, personalized work space.

❖ **Storage.** Things, things, and more things—where can you put them all? Think outside the box—the plastic black in-box, that is. Try baskets for files, books, even supplies. For a printer stand, consider using an old bench painted in the shade of your choice. An armoire (snagged on superclearance, of course) can house all your office supplies, and your filing cabinet can get an easy makeover if you toss a beautiful tablecloth over it. Business cards don't have to be slipped into a boring card file. I keep mine in a whimsical coffee mug a friend gave me one Christmas. They're neat, organized alphabetically, and always within reach.

Illustration 10-C. An improvised bulletin board.

What's Your Office Type?

The reasons for setting up a home office are as varied as the individuals who set them up. But there are some common home office types, and what you need will likely fall into one (or more) of these categories:

Home Office on the Cheap

You *want* a home office. You may even *need* a home office. One trip to the office supply store and you may think this is going to be an expensive project, but it doesn't have to be. In fact, even on the tightest of budgets, you can set up a productive home office in your apartment where you can accomplish everything you need to, and you can do it all in style.

Jeff Zbar has worked as a home-based journalist and author since the 1980s. He specializes in work-at-home, teleworking, alternative officing, and small business marketing, technology, communications, and motivation. If you want to assemble a low-budget home office, he suggests the following:

- Look at your intended workspace. Envision creative ways to use it—without buying a large desk or traditional work surface that would consume more space in the home office.

- Think about what you can do with scrap lumber, a couple of used filing cabinets, and an old door.

- Affix a new coat of paint, inexpensive laminate, or even fabric trim to the top of the work surface to help enliven and renew its appearance.

- Attach a strip of Velcro to the edge of a make-shift desk and the other strip to a piece of fabric. Then drape the fabric around the edge of the work surface. Filing cabinets, other storage pieces, and even the office chair can be hidden away beneath the desk when not in use.

- Check used office furniture stores or office equipment leasing companies for ample desks and chairs to choose from. Quality filing cabinets might be more difficult to find. Shop around for price and quality.

- Visit the local thrift or consignment shop for used furniture and equipment.

- Read the classified ads for furniture sales, auctions, or liquidations.

☉ Know anyone in a business? Check around. Sometimes businesses preparing to upgrade their furniture will part with it cheaply.

☉ Hit a local retailer to find out when they're going to replace their display furnishings, which often make good, sturdy office hardware.

Jeff Zbar is the author of Your Profitable Home Business Made E-Z, Home Office Know-How *and* Home Office Success Stories, *a free e-zine you can read about at www.chiefhomeofficer.com.*

The "Running the Household" Home Office

You'll likely need basic equipment such as a computer, a printer, and perhaps a scanner. Computer desks come in a variety of shapes and sizes, in a wide range of prices. I picked up my first computer desk at a yard sale for $20. It was a cheap, ugly wood (actually, it was particle board) that I painted and used for years, then sold it at my own garage sale for $25. If you work at your computer regularly, invest in a desk that is designed for computer use—one that includes a keyboard shelf or drawer. After my own painful bout with carpal tunnel syndrome, I can assure you any investment in ergonomically correct furnishings is well worth it.

If you can't find the desk you want in your price range, don't despair. You can create your own as a temporary (or even permanent) solution. You'll need two filing cabinets and a piece of wood for the top. You can purchase a sliding keyboard drawer from an office supply store and attach it easily for comfortable typing.

Second, you'll need a place to store bills and other household papers. A metal filing cabinet is a great choice that will last many years, and you can always find one for a good price at an office supply or discount store. (And they can be painted easily!)

The Parents' and Kids' Work Home Office

You'll also probably have basic computer equipment, a scanner, and a printer. If kids and parents use the same computer and desk, be sure to purchase a chair that will raise and lower to each user's height. Flea markets are a great place to hunt for these, as are going-out-of-business sales. Also check your newspaper classified advertisements for businesses that are liquidating office chairs. Furniture rental companies are great places to call about such sales, too.

When selecting furnishings for this type of home office, always keep *access* in mind. If adults and kids use reference materials, keep the bookshelves low so children can be self-sufficient in the space. If you opt for taller bookcases, use the lower shelves for reference books, paper and supplies all users need, and higher shelves for supplies you'd like to keep out of children's reach, such as potentially messy toner cartridges. Try stashing supplies in ceramic bowls, hat boxes, and even beautiful antique suitcases.

This type of home office is also a good place for a family calendar center. You can place a paper calendar (or any type of calendar) or dry erase board in a central location where anyone in the family can add events to it.

The Heavy-Duty Crafter's Home Office

You'll need ample shelving and storage space in the crafter's home office. Clear plastic shoe boxes are always a good choice, because you can place them on shelves and see what's in them without having to pull them down and open each one.

You might also want to keep some of your creations on hand for display. For instance, if you're a rubber-stamp crafter, you may want to hold onto the original cards you create, so you can use them as templates later. Years ago, I saw a great tip in a decorating magazine: Buy a roll of inexpensive cork board at your hardware or home improvement store and attach it to your wall as a chair-rail-height border. (Check with your landlord first, if you think he or she might object or if your lease prohibits this.) You can tack your creations or anything you wish to display onto this functional border. This keeps those items accessible when you need them, and when you don't, they create a decorative room accent. If plain cork board on a wall seems a little plain for your taste, try adding wood trim or wallpaper border running along the top and bottom of the cork board.

If you're working in a basement or other room lacking architectural character, try putting inspiration under your feet. Floor cloths are inexpensive and easy to create with just canvas and acrylic paints.

The Telecommuter's (or Home-Based Business) Home Office

If you work at home full- or part-time, you have plenty of company. Recent research estimates vary widely, but some say as many as fifty million people in the United States alone work at least part-time at home. And that number continues to grow each year.

This type of home office can have very significant needs, and those needs can vary greatly from person to person, according to your job and what you must accomplish in your home office.

At the very least, you'll probably need a computer, a printer, a desk and a chair, a telephone, and shelving. You may also need a fax machine, scanner, a photocopier, a speaker phone, and other electronic office equipment. And if you meet with clients or coworkers at home, you may need some sort of large table for conferences or project work. If your meetings are not frequent, a dining room table should work just fine for this use. And since your dining room is probably in the main living area in your apartment (unlike a spare bedroom), coworkers and clients may feel comfortable there.

For your desk and chair, consider comfort, convenience, and ergonomic safety above all else, particularly if you'll spend long hours working there. Other furnishings, such as filing cabinets and bookshelves, can be picked up secondhand for substantial savings.

If you use your home office daily, you might find it difficult to keep the general area neat. If you're in a separate room that has a door, this might not be too much of a problem. But if you're in a section of a main living area, you can utilize room dividers or screens so when you're off duty, your work area is not always in your view. Curtains suspended from the ceiling is another creative, inexpensive option that's easy to remove if you change your mind.

Ideas, Tips, and Tricks

✣ To brighten up a kid's room for very little money, suspend a kite from the ceiling with fishing wire.

✣ Want to avoid being interrupted by roommates or family members when you're working in your home office? Make a simple, reversible sign to help you out! On one side write, "Working—Please Do Not Disturb," and on the other write, "Come on In." Hang the sign on a doorknob, a room divider, or even the back of your chair.

chapter 11

Storage

Storage space is an elusive concept, and the "perfect" amount is often just a little more than we have. The right amount of storage is like a carrot always dangling before us. And no matter what we do, it seems impossible to reach it.

Many of us equate "space"—such as closets—with storage. "If I just had one more closet," we say, "then my storage needs would be covered." Or we buy lots of plastic containers or other items traditionally associated with storage, thinking that if we buy enough of them, our problem just might be solved.

I believe the answer lies not in more plastic containers but in thinking about storage more creatively. Many of us believe that most of our things should be contained and hidden or, at the very least, put away. But you don't really need to hide your belongings unless you want to. If you're worried that storing things in plain view will look messy or cluttered, I assure you, there are many ways to avoid falling into that trap. Also, wouldn't it be great not to have to hunt for your winter coat, your roller skates, or extra bed sheets when you need them? The key is this: You need to create inexpensive, accessible storage solutions. I like to call it smart storage.

Creative Containment

When you have items that you need to store, do you automatically reach for cardboard boxes and stuff them until they are overflowing? While cardboard boxes might be fine for storing some items, they are not a very attractive solution, and for this reason, things stored this way tend to get pushed to the back of a closet where no one can see them—not even you. But what happens when you need something that's in the box? You'll have to move all your shoes and other items that get piled up around the boxes, and dig through to find what you're looking for. Does this sound like your system? It's the system I used for years until I realized there are better ways to store things!

If you've never considered storing your belongings in style, perhaps it's time! The type of creative containment you opt for depends on several factors. First, you'll need to consider what you're storing. Clothing, for instance, should be treated differently than garden tools. Second, consider the location and the environmental factors of that location. If you have an unused computer you're storing, you'll want a location that won't get too cold or too damp, since these conditions could damage the computer. Third, you can begin thinking about the containers you'll use. Although plastic bins and cardboard boxes can get the job done, consider these more creative alternatives:

For Long-Term Storage

❖ Instead of banishing sweaters or off-season clothing to the back of your closet or stashing them in cardboard, try something different. Pick up old drawers at a flea market, paint or stain them to match or complement your bed, then add four rolling casters on the bottom so it can be moved around easily. Store each unit under your bed, and you're putting a little-used space to a productive use.

❖ Tired of a linen closet that's overflowing? Purchase an inexpensive wicker hamper and store off-season linens in a closet. Beach towels can occupy the hamper in the winter, and flannel sheets can hibernate there during the summer.

Short-Term Storage

◎ If you're short on bathroom space, use decorative hooks to hold baskets or bags full of toiletries (see example in illustration 11-A).

◎ Small shelves mounted over doorways or windows can hold items like books and collectibles.

◎ Shoe bags are versatile receptacles that can store a multitude of things, from Beanie Baby collections to craft supplies to correspondence.

◎ Small items (e.g., buttons, safety pins, etc.) can be stored in bulk easily. Purchase a few matching glass jars with screw-on lids. Glue the lids onto the bottom side of wall shelf, with the lids in a straight line with a few inches between them. Fill the jars with small items, and screw the jars on the lids (see example in illustration 11-B). When you need a button, grab the jar and twist, retrieve it, then screw it back into place.

Illustration 11-A. Decorative hooks with baskets to hold toiletries.

◉ Another idea for storing lots of small items: Remove the label from an old paint can, paint the can all one color, and decorate it with decoupage or paint markers. Use the cans to store belts, game pieces like dominoes, small toys, photos—anything! Glue several paint cans together for an interesting storage unit.

Storage for Everything

Professional organizers expound the virtues of finding a place for everything. It seems that the clutter that takes over our lives is caused by items that really don't belong *somewhere*. Hence, they are simply left *anywhere*.

So when you're attempting to find suitable storage for belongings, your first step will be to get organized. Begin by purging yourself of the things you don't need or don't want. Although many people won't place things they don't want on display in their home, many will tuck these very same items into drawers or closets, just in case. However, since storage space in many apartments is limited, it's important to stay focused and store away only items you know you will need at some point.

In addition, there are many things we must hold onto, even though we'd rather not. Receipts, tax returns, and other personal papers are examples. You may not need these items often, but you will probably need them sooner or later. But not all items that require storage are seldom used. There are many often-used things in our homes that need a place to "live" so when we need them, we know just where to look.

Here are some creative ways to find a home for many of the things that make their way into our homes:

Magazines

❖ Cut the top off of old cereal boxes and cover the rest of the box with Con-Tact paper, wallpaper, or other decorative surface.

❖ Store magazines in a tin bucket for a look that is great with Country, Traditional, or even Contemporary interiors.

Personal Papers

◎ Expandable, multipocket file folders are inexpensive, compact, easy to find, and keep papers neatly organized by the categories of your choosing.

Illustration 11-B. Jars glued underneath a wall-mounted shelf to store small items.

◎ Create a personal notebook by purchasing a large binder and pocket folder dividers. Use it to store phone lists, invitations, prescription and medical information, warranties, stamps, stationery, and any papers you need to access on a regular basis. (But remember to clean it out now and then.)

◎ Cover old shoeboxes (including the lid) with decorative paper, write the contents on the end of the box, and then stack them on a closet shelf.

◎ Photo albums, memory albums, and photo boxes are all great choices for storing photos. For photos you'd like to share more often, place them in a ceramic or wooden bowl and make them part of a tabletop grouping in your living room.

Bills and Correspondence

✣ Create a portable correspondence center by using a wine box or wooden crate with containers of various sizes placed inside. A wooden "toolbox" from a crafts store also works great and already has built-in dividers so you won't need extra containers.

✣ Purchase an inexpensive expanding file folder with at least five or six sections. Label each section to correspond with a week of the month, like this: "First Week of Month," "Second Week of Month," and so forth. When a bill arrives, slip it into the section for the week you plan to pay it. At the beginning of each week, check the folder and see what's due.

Books

☉ Purchase square or rectangular wicker, wire, metal, or wooden containers to hold smaller books. This will help keep them conveniently together, and the container looks orderly when placed on exposed shelving.

☉ If you have many large books, stack them on the floor to create a small night table next to your bed.

Clothing and Linens

✣ Store linens neatly folded in laundry baskets or hampers.

✣ Roll up towels, sheets, or blankets, and store them in baskets under tables.

✣ Place them in a trunk that's being used as a coffee table, at the foot of a bed, as a side table, or as benchlike seating.

Kitchen Storage

- Place cooking utensils in porcelain or ceramic bowls, vases, pitchers, and mugs (see example in illustration 11-C).

- Hang (or nail) a piece of lattice on the wall and add hooks for hanging things like pots, pans, pot holders, towels, and even large cooking utensils. It's inexpensive and removable and stops these items from scratching up your kitchen wall. (And you'll free up drawer and cabinet space.)

- Keep spices in matching, simple glass containers (like Ball jars), and they'll be so attractive you can leave them right out on the counter. (For smaller quantities, baby food jars work great, too.)

Illustration 11-C. A decorative ceramic pitcher holds cooking utensils.

Making Closets Smarter

A professional organizer once told me that investing in a closet organization system is one of the wisest investments you could ever make. And I agree! Shoe racks, shelf dividers, multilevel rods, and other features make closet systems invaluable for organization and optimization of storage space. If you're in the market for a closet system, be sure to follow these tips:

- Measure your closet carefully before heading out to purchase a system.
- Shop around for sales and get the best system you can afford.

Smart Clothing Closets on a Budget

We expect a lot from closets. We want them to not only hold the items we use, but they also must hold the things we rarely need and even some things we just don't want to see. And we want our closets to do both of these jobs at the same time. Is it any wonder that many of us have closets that don't look perfectly neat and tidy?

Our poor closets are caught in a catch-22: we need for them to be neat and efficient because of everything we put in them, but because of everything we put in them, they cannot remain neat and efficient.

A disorganized clothing closet is much more than an eyesore—it can cause you to lose time (looking for things), money (buying things you thought you needed but didn't), and perhaps even lose your mind. Okay, maybe you won't lose your mind, but a disastrous clothing closet certainly can be a stressful place to begin your day.

If your closet space is very limited (and many apartment dwellers deal with this reality), the easiest option is to rotate your wardrobe by season. In other words, only clothing that can be worn in the current season may claim a space in your clothing closet. Off-season clothing is stored away somewhere else until you need it. (But remember, if you're storing clothing and linens, place some cedar strips or cedar balls in the container to ward off moths.)

Additional clothing closet dos include these:

❖ Try to keep everything in plain sight, and getting dressed will be easier. (One exception to this rule—place shoes in boxes on a high shelf, take a photo of the pair, and secure it to the front of the box so you don't have to rifle through several boxes just to find your dress navy blue pumps.

❖ Purge first! You know the old rule: If you haven't worn it in the last year, you probably won't ever wear it again, so get rid of it!

* Purchase shelf dividers if you're folding items and placing them on wide closet shelves. This keeps things neatly corralled into their appropriate spots.

* Place jewelry, socks, and hosiery in hanging cosmetic travel bags (the ones with lots of pockets and a clear window in front.) Hang these right on your closet rod or from a hook on a wall or on the back of your door.

* If you have an empty section of wall in your closet, use it! Attach plenty of hooks (screw in or removable adhesive) for purses, belts, scarves, and other items that often get lost in closets (see example in illustration 11-D).

* If you're renting, make sure your system is easily removable and won't require huge holes or other things that may get you into trouble with your landlord.

If your clothing closets came equipped with a wire closet system, you're in luck! If the closet system's setup is not perfect for you, you can purchase individual pieces of systems that will work with your current setup.

Where to Shop for Storage Solutions

If you're looking for traditional storage items, there are plenty of places to shop. Stores like Kmart, Wal-Mart, and Target have large selections for reasonable prices, and home improvement stores are great places to shop for complete closet-organizing systems.

If you're looking for items with a little more personality, huge selections or specialty items you can't find elsewhere, check out these great Web sites:

* **The Container Store**–www.thecontainerstore.com. This is one of my very favorite stores, and their Web site is great, too. They carry every conceivable organizing product, plus a bunch you'd never even think of.

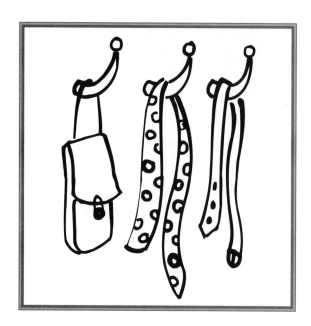

Illustration 11-D. Hooks in a closet to hold smaller accessories.

⊚ **Hold Everything**—www.hold everything.com. Some of their products cost a bit more than I like to spend, but they have great style and a very nice selection. (It's no wonder—they're owned by specialty retailer Williams Sonoma, Inc., the company that also owns Pottery Barn.)

⊚ **Stacks and Stacks**—www.stacks andstacks.com. I found them recently and was immediately hooked on their convenient, easy-to-use Web site. Their selection ranges from inexpensive, bare-bones bins and boxes to classic wood furniture.

Ideas, Tips, and Tricks

❖ Vintage metal beach pails make great containers for holding pencils, pens, paintbrushes, and other such items.

❖ Need to store shoes (e.g., outdoor shoes) in a room that doesn't have a closet? Try stashing them in a wicker picnic basket or any basket with a lid. The wicker lets the shoes "breathe," and the lid keeps the pile from becoming an eyesore.

❖ Purchase a set of old school lockers from a flea market to hold sports equipment or tools.

chapter **12**

Making Your Apartment Your Home

Home is where the heart is. Home is where you hang your hat. Home sweet home.

There are a thousand sentiments about homes that we've all heard many times. But most focus on a simple concept: that your home is a special and even sacred place. It is the place where you begin and end your day, where you rest, love, laugh, cry, and do much of the living that life is all about. Given the incredible importance of this place, making it suit your taste and your lifestyle is important, don't you think?

Your Perfect Apartment Home

Apartments, condominiums, townhouses, duplexes, lofts–they're all places that millions of Americans call home. Hopefully, your apartment is a place you *like* to call home. If it isn't, I hope this book will help you change that, at least in some small way.

If you live in a place that doesn't feel right to you, I encourage you to look around, reflect on your space, and try to identify what's really bothering you about it. Is it the neighborhood, building, or apartment complex that troubles you? Is it the apartment itself, the floor plan, the colors of the walls, or the size of the rooms? There are many reasons why an apartment might fall short of your ideal, and some of them can't be changed. But some of them can.

Working With Your Decorating Budget

If you're reading this book, you're probably an apartment dweller with a tight decorating budget, either by choice or by necessity, or a little of both. There's certainly nothing wrong with having a tight budget, but notice there's a very important word at work here: *budget.* To decorate or redecorate your apartment for optimal results, you need to identify your budget as soon as possible. Your budget will likely begin with a single number (which you may break down into categories later). It may be $100, $500, $1,000, or more, depending on what you need to do and how you'd like to do it. Whatever that budget figure is, *claim* that number—it's yours. You don't even have to share that number with anyone else if you don't want to. But you must know it. You must repeat it to yourself; write it down; think about it each time you hit a garage sale, furniture store, or Web site in search of furnishings or accessories. Of course, there may be times when you must exceed your budget, and that's okay! No one wants you to pass up a collectible you've been scouting for years or a print that makes you weep because you want it so much. But these should be infrequent occurrences.

In the first chapters of this book, I encouraged you to determine your decorating goals, draw up a budget worksheet, and get organized. It seems like a lengthy process, I know. You may be thinking, "Gee, I just want to make a few changes. I'll just go out and see what strikes my fancy." I've been there many times. But if you're hoping to do more than just buy a sofa or make a simple change or two, you may want to think it out more carefully. I've redecorated with no budget pinpointed, no goals in mind, and clutter filling every corner of most rooms. I figured I was just too busy to take a detailed approach to decorating, so I'd just wing it. Everything would be fine because I knew my style, and I knew what to look for and where to find it. Need I tell you how very wrong I was?

I ended up spending much more than I should have, I had too many accessories and not enough furnishings, and I made several large impulse purchases I later regretted. In addition, I simply "forgot" some important items. Don't get the wrong idea—I did do some things right! But without a plan, you're not as likely to do a great job of staying on your budget and getting exactly what you want and need. So even if you don't fill out all the worksheets included in the first chapter, please remember this: Determining your budget and knowing your goals are critical.

Everyone Can Think Creatively

As a budget decorating writer, I receive lots of e-mail from people who have a decorating dilemma and are seeking advice. Some of them are so desperate when they write. They plead with me, "Please help me! I've tried everything!" Many of them also mention that they want very much to decorate their rooms beautifully on a budget, but they're not "the creative type." Sometimes they write things like "I just can't do that. I don't know how!"

Sure, crafters might have an advantage over noncrafters when it comes to dreaming up ways to decorate on a budget. But even people who don't believe they have a creative bone in their body can come up with wonderful, inventive ideas for decorating their space. Decorating success has just as much to do with keeping your eyes open for ideas and looking at things in new and exciting ways than it does the tendency to be artistic. So whether you're a CPA, a schoolteacher, or a decorative painter doesn't really matter. What matters is how good a job you want to do decorating your apartment and how much time and energy you're willing to invest in it.

So as you embark on your budget decorating adventures, give yourself credit for being able to do a great job, even before you start. Your confidence will lead you to take risks, and it will open up possibilities you might never have had if you felt scared or unable to tackle the job.

Does Decorating Ever End?

I am always moving things around, from room to room, or even just around the same room. I get a little antsy when things stay in the same place for too long. I need something new and exciting to look at, and since my decorating budget is (and probably always will be) modest, I can't buy new stuff whenever I want a change. So instead I rearrange. Rearranging is the ideal way to make changes when you have no budget at all.

When you have a little money to spend, you can make small investments go a long way. A tabletop grouping you're getting tired of can be refreshed with the addition of a few pillar candles in interesting hues. This change can be accomplished for just a few dollars per pillar, and you can even get the scented kind that come with an aromatic touch. A framed print that looks a little boring can take on a more exciting life with a new frame or even just a paint job on its original frame. Think small changes that create a big impact. I once changed the look of a very large living room wall by adding a single item above my sofa: a $30 piece of architectural salvage that was about three feet wide and a foot deep. The piece has so much character, it has become a conversation piece and focal point, and most friends who walk into the room immediately say, "Hey, something's different in here. What did you do?"

When you want a change and you have little to spend, focus on accessories. Hit the fabric store and get a few yards of a bright, funky ribbon, and make new curtain tiebacks for any room that needs a kick. Buy colored lightbulbs and change a room simply by refining the lighting. Get your grandmother's old quilt out of the closet and drape it over a boring sofa. Bring books off your bookshelves and use them to add height to displays. Look around, think, try things out. What have you really got to lose, anyway?

Include the Right People in Your Decorating

Does it really matter if your next-door neighbor doesn't like the way you've arranged your kitchen? Well, no offense, but not really. Sure you might want a second opinion, and that's great. But when you're decorating, make sure you include all the *right* people in the decision making. Got a roommate? Make sure they can live with the decorating decisions you're making. You don't have to agree with one another on every single detail. In fact, that probably would be impossible. But as you begin to decorate, or better yet, *before* you move in together, sit down and discuss the types of living environment you both like. If your styles are extremely different with little common ground, it may be a tough road. But keep trying until you reach a compromise. In cases of completely opposite tastes, perhaps each of you can decorate certain areas as you wish, and you may both agree to live with that.

If you have a spouse or partner, make sure you're both involved in major buys, especially furniture purchases. Of course, you won't be together when finding every item that goes into your apartment. But make sure you've checked in with your partner before you drag home a $500 sofa. Even if you love the sofa and think it's the most beautiful piece of furniture ever made, if your mate hates it, it's probably going to be a sore spot, at least once in a while. You're also showing respect for your partner by including him or her in these joint purchases, because it lets this special person know you care about what he or she wants, too.

If you have children, it's tempting to decorate their rooms in a way that makes sense to you. Try to resist this temptation. Although you, as the parent, will make the final decisions, involve your child as much as possible. Let them pick out the main colors of the room and take part in as much of the decorating as they can, depending on their age. If they're babies or toddlers, keep their room simple;

as they get older, they'll have more opportunities for injecting their own personality into the room's decor. And try to stay away from themes that focus on currently popular cartoon characters, toys, or movies. They become outdated quickly.

Now, Take a Deep Breath and Begin!

If you are feeling a little worried about what lies of head of you, that's understandable. But don't ignore it if the anxiety is strong. Decorating should be a fun, exciting adventure, not a painful event. If you're feeling very tense about the whole thing, take a step back and try to determine why. Is the budget you're working with too high? Are you in the middle of life changes that make it hard for you to focus on this task? Are you unhappy with your roommate and therefore find it difficult to work on the living spaces you share? If you have such problems, put off major decorating for a while. Working on your apartment might seem like a good diversion to help you forget about an unhappy condition, but the issues that are really bothering you will have to be worked out sooner or later.

When you're ready to begin decorating your apartment, you will probably start noticing things like interesting groupings in friends' homes, or perhaps you'll impulsively pick up a decorating magazine (or two, or three) in the grocery store. When the time is right, you'll know, and you'll do a much better job if the stress has been worked through.

Another idea, if you're not feeling confident about decorating, is to get advice from professionals. Many interior decorators across the country specialize in providing design services for small-budget clients. Some friends of mine contacted one such designer, who came to their home for just a few hours and gave them many ideas on how to improve problems areas. Her consultation fee was reasonable, and they were able to initiate her ideas all by themselves.

The difference, in some rooms, was incredible, and their money was well spent.

You can get free help, too. There are many Web sites and television programs dedicated to decorating. Seek them out and see whether they can help you. Jot down ideas, print out instructions—don't go it alone; there's plenty of help out there.

Most of all, I encourage you to have fun while you decorate your living spaces, no matter what your budget may be. Good luck!

RESOURCES

RETAIL STORES AND CATALOG SHOPPING

American Home Stencils
(800) 742-4520
www.americanhomestencils.com

Bed, Bath and Beyond
(800) 462-3966
www.bedbathandbeyond.com

The Company Store
(800) 285-DOWN
www.thecompanystore.com

Dressler Stencil Company, Inc.
(888) 656-4515
www.dresslerstencils.com

Kmart
(866) KMART4U
www.kmart.com

Mohawk Carpet
Dalton, Georgia
(800) 2MOHAWK
www.mohawkcarpet.com

The Purple Cow
2500 Sandy Plains Road
Marietta, Georgia 30066
(770) 579-6828
E-mail: thepurplecow@msn.com

Surefit (slipcovers)
(888) SURE FIT
www.surefit.com

Target
(888) 304-4000
www.target.com

Wal-Mart
(800) WAL-MART
www.walmart.com

BOOKS

Better Homes and Gardens Flea Market Decorating, ed. Vicki L. Ingham (Meredith Books, 2000).

Decorating on a Dime by Christy Ferer (Warner Books, 1997).

Mary Emmerling's Quick Decorating by Jill Kirchner and Michael Skott (Clarkson Potter, 1997).

The Official Directory of U.S. Flea Markets, 7th ed., ed. Kitty Werner (Ballantine, 2000).

Rachel Ashwell's Shabby Chic Treasure Hunting & Decorating Guide by Rachel Ashwell (ReganBooks, HarperCollins, 1998).

U.S. Flea Market Directory: A Guide to the Best Flea Markets in All 50 States (U.S. Flea Market Directory) by Albert Lafarge (St. Martin's Press, 2000).

Use What You Have Decorating by Lauri Ward (Penguin Putnam, 1998)

WEB SITES

Supplies

The Internet Wallpaper Store
www.wallpaperstore.com

Joann.com
www.joann.com

Wallies Wallpaper Cutouts
www.wallies.com

General Decorating and Projects

Decorating Your Home
www.decorating-your-home.com

Decorator Secrets
www.decoratorsecrets.com

The Everyday Decorator
www.everydaydecorator.com

Home and Garden Television
www.hgtv.com

HomeDecoratingSite.com
www.4homedecoratingsite.com

LivingandEntertaining.com
www.livingandentertaining.com

Wallflowers.net
www.wallflowers.net

Women.com's Home & Garden Site
hg.women.com

Budget Decorating

Goddess of Garbage
Carol A. Tanzi, A.S.I.D.
www.goddessofgarbage.com

Suite 101 Budget Decorating
www.suite101.com/welcome.cfm/bud
get_decorating

Online Shopping

Remember, too, that many department, discount, and furniture stores have their own Web sites these days; try typing in their name with ".com" at the end for starters.

The Container Store
www.thecontainerstore.com

eBay
www.ebay.com

ihome.com
www.ihome.com

IKEA
www.ikea.com

Getting Organized and Cleaning

Amet's Essentials
(Aromatherapy products)
(877) 328-6663
www.ametsessentials.com

Duncan Resource Group, Inc.
Peggy Duncan, CEO
www.duncanresource.com

Organizedhome.com
www.organizedhome.com

Apartment Resources

Apartment.com
www.apartment.com

Homestore.com Apartments
  & Rentals
www.springstreet.com/apartments

FLEA MARKETS AND ANTIQUE SHOPPING

On the Web

FleaMarketGuide.com
www.fleamarketguide.com

Yardsale.com
www.yardsale.com

Around the United States

Historic Lakewood Antiques Market
Lakewood Fairgrounds
1-75, I-85 Exit 88 East
Atlanta, GA
(404) 622-4488
Second weekend of each month

Brimfield Outdoor Antiques and
Collectibles Show
Brimfield, MA
www.brimfieldshow.com
Held three times a year

The Highway 127 Corridor Sale
(a.k.a. The World's Longest Outdoor
Yard Sale)
Runs 450 Miles along U.S. Highway
127, from Gadsden, Alabama, to
Covington, Kentucky
www.127sale.com

Hints, Tips, and Worksheets

There are many random parts to decorating that can make you feel frazzled. I've included some organizational tips and worksheets to help get you on the right track when it comes to terminology, moving, entertaining, troubleshooting, and more.

Feel free to copy pages from this section so you can use these forms more than once. File them in your decorating notebook for quick reference.

Hints, Tips, and Worksheets Contents

Helpful Terms

ACCENT WALL: One wall in a room painted a different color than the other walls.

AROMATHERAPY: The ancient art of using essential oils (see essential oils definition) to heal the mind, body, and spirit.

BEAD BOARD: A type of wood paneling that appears as long, thin strips of wood separated by grooves.

BED IN A BAG: A comforter, sheets, pillowcases, bed skirt, and shams sold together as a set.

BISTRO SET: A small table and chairs used for dining.

CHAIR RAIL: A strip of molding attached to a wall and located at the approximate height of the back of a chair.

CLOSET ORGANIZING SYSTEM: A pre-packaged set of tools designed to fit into your closet. Sets typically include multilevel rods, shelving, shoe trees, and other pieces.

COLOR WHEEL: A device often used by designers to help them make color combination choices. The wheel shows primary, secondary, and tertiary colors.

COMPLEMENTARY COLORS: Colors found opposite each other on a color wheel (see color wheel definition).

CONSIGNMENT SHOP: A store that sells previously owned items, then pays the original owner after the item has sold.

CORBEL: A bracket made from wood, stone, brick, or other material, used for support in architecture.

DECORATING GOALS STATEMENT: A statement that outlines your ultimate goals, hopes, and desires in decorating your home.

DECORATING NOTEBOOK: A notebook that holds decorating ideas, such as magazine clippings, paint and wallpaper samples, photographs, and project instructions.

DECOUPAGE: Adhering photos, postcards, or other decorative paper items to a surface and covering the decorated surface area with varnish.

ESSENTIAL OIL: Natural oil extracted from plants, flowers, herbs, and trees used in aromatherapy.

ESTATE SALE: An event designed to sell a person's belongings, often held after a person dies.

FAUX PAINTING: Faux means "false" in French. Faux painting provides the illusion of texture (such as with combing) or other type of surface (such as faux marble).

FOLK ART: Artwork created by persons not trained or educated in the creation of art.

FLOORCLOTH: A decorative floor covering created with heavy canvas and paint.

FOCAL POINT: A strong point of interest in a room.

KEYBOARD DRAWER: A drawer attached to a table or desk to hold a computer keyboard. Often slides in and out under the desktop, and can improve the ergonomic setup of a computer work area.

LATTICE: Wood strips crisscrossed or interwoven to create a panel.

STENCIL: A design cut into a piece of material (typically plastic) that is placed on a surface so paint can be applied to it, transferring the design to the surface.

SWAP MEET: Another name for a flea market.

Project Organizer

By now your head may be spinning with many ideas for decorating projects—at least I hope it is! Sometimes it can be difficult to keep track of what you want to do when you have the time and money to work on your apartment. This project organizer contains worksheets that will help you record your ideas and important information, so when you're ready to tackle a project, you'll be off and running!

Living Room

Project: _____   **Budget:** _____

Tools

_____   _____

_____   _____

_____   _____

_____   _____

Materials

_____   _____

_____   _____

_____   _____

_____   _____

Ideas

_____   _____

_____   _____

_____   _____

_____   _____

Measurements

Room width _____   Room length _____

Window width _____   Window length _____

Window width _____   Window length _____

Window width _____   Window length _____

Priority (circle one): HIGH   MEDIUM   LOW

Kitchen

Project: _____   **Budget:** _____

Tools

_____   _____

_____   _____

_____   _____

_____   _____

Materials

_____   _____

_____   _____

_____   _____

_____   _____

Ideas

_____   _____

_____   _____

_____   _____

_____   _____

Measurements

Room width _____   Room length _____

Window width _____   Window length _____

Window width _____   Window length _____

Window width _____   Window length _____

Priority (circle one): HIGH   MEDIUM   LOW

Bedroom

Project: _____   **Budget:** _____

Tools

_____   _____
_____   _____
_____   _____
_____   _____

Materials

_____   _____
_____   _____
_____   _____
_____   _____

Ideas

_____   _____
_____   _____
_____   _____
_____   _____

Measurements

Room width _____   Room length _____
Window width _____   Window length _____
Window width _____   Window length _____
Window width _____   Window length _____

Priority (circle one): HIGH   MEDIUM   LOW

Bathroom

Project: _____ **Budget:** _____

Tools

_____   _____

_____   _____

_____   _____

_____   _____

Materials

_____   _____

_____   _____

_____   _____

_____   _____

Ideas

_____   _____

_____   _____

_____   _____

_____   _____

Measurements

Room width _____   Room length _____

Window width _____   Window length _____

Window width _____   Window length _____

Window width _____   Window length _____

Priority (circle one): HIGH   MEDIUM   LOW

Other Room: _____

Project: _____ **Budget:** _____

Tools

_____   _____

_____   _____

_____   _____

_____   _____

Materials

_____   _____

_____   _____

_____   _____

_____   _____

Ideas

_____   _____

_____   _____

_____   _____

_____   _____

Measurements

Room width _____   Room length _____

Window width _____   Window length _____

Window width _____   Window length _____

Window width _____   Window length _____

Priority (circle one): HIGH   MEDIUM   LOW

Decorating Troubleshooting Guide

Do you have a decorating dilemma? It's not the end of the world! In fact, many people probably have the very same problem, and there are likely many ways to fix it.

Check the Troubleshooting Guide that follows to locate possible solutions to your decorating problems.

Furnishings and Accessories

Sparse Furnishings and Accessories

Add a large, inexpensive item (e.g., an oversized plant); group smaller items together and they will look more substantial; hang large items like decorative quilts, blankets, or rugs on the wall. Or simply decide to enjoy a streamlined, minimalist look!

Old, Worn Furnishings

Use paint or slipcovers to revive furnishings that are showing age or badly worn. Painting wood furniture (e.g., end tables) the same color as the walls and placing them against the walls will make them less noticeable. Also, use items like buttons, fringe, and ribbon to embellish furniture and accessories and make them more interesting.

A New Living Room or Bedroom "Look"

For a living room, purchase (or re-cover) pillows; add an inexpensive throw; change (or dye) your curtains. For a bedroom, purchase (or sew) new pillow cases, and stick with a neutral bedspread, so you can change the look inexpensively whenever you like.

Colors and Mood

Toning Down a Room

Soothe the room with neutral colors in small rugs, pillows, blankets, and window treatments. Remove some items, such as those with colors that clash with other items in the room, and send them to another room.

Livening Up a Room

Color can help make a room less boring, as can texture. Try painting the room, an accent wall, or your molding in a new color to wake up a boring room. A new piece of artwork in a prominent position or several plants can also help. To bring in texture, add items like a jute or sisal rug or wicker baskets.

Making a Room Comfortable

Determine what causes the discomfort. Is it the flow of the room? The positioning of the furniture? Rearrange until you get it right. If you still can't determine the problem, empty the room as much as possible and begin again with a clean slate. Also bring accessories and furnishings from other rooms to see whether you can find a better fit here.

"Balancing" a Room

It could be a problem with the "height" or "weight" of some of your furnishings and accessories. Try not to lump all the small items with small items and large items with large. Spread out what you have, and if you have a tall item on one side of a piece of furniture or a fireplace mantel, place another one of more or less equal height on the opposite side.

Modernizing Your Kitchen

Many apartment kitchens are outdated. If your cabinets are wood, check with your landlord to see whether he'll permit you to paint them. You can also paint countertops; a faux technique, such as marbelizing, is a great choice for this job.

For quick pick-me-ups in outdated kitchens, try new cabinet knobs and drawer pulls, new kitchen towels and small rugs, or a ceiling-mounted pot rack holding potted plants with vines that drape down. Or add a "backsplash" using a wallpaper border or paint one on using stencils or rubber stamps.

Sprucing Up Walls

Add the illusion of texture and depth to your walls by using a faux painting technique such as sponging or combing. Adding a stenciled border can also make your walls more interesting.

If you can't (or don't want to) paint, try using fabric to liven up your walls. Hang panels or interesting fabrics in strips on large expanses of walls or behind your sofa. You can also hang netting behind the head of your bed for a soft, romantic look.

Get rid of the hooks, nails, and screws that are currently used to hang your artwork. Replace them with interesting knobs and hooks, and you won't even have to replace the artwork to still get a great new look.

Architectural Problems

Low Ceiling

Lift your ceiling (or make it look like you did) by painting it a light, airy color. For more drama and lift, paint it light blue and sponge on fluffy clouds using a sea sponge and white paint.

If you don't want to paint, simply stack artwork (one above the other) on the wall to draw the eyes upward. Also sprinkle "tall" items through your apartment, such as indoor trees, ladders, and floor lamps.

Few (or Small) Windows

Add mirrors strategically in your apartment so they reflect the light from the few windows that you have. Make small windows appear larger by suspending their curtains from the ceiling to the floor, no matter what the actual window size may be. Add windows by hanging old, salvaged stained glass (or regular) windows on window-free walls. A grouping of several salvaged windows in various styles also looks great.

Flooring in Poor Condition

Cover old, ugly flooring with an ample-sized sisal or jute area rug. You can also paint old wood or linoleum flooring. (See chapter 3 for more information.)

For worn-out carpeting, try a good steam cleaning and then cover with one large or several small area rugs. A floorcloth is an inexpensive way to get the exact size and colors you want in a floor covering, and you can do it yourself. (See chapter 3 for floorcloths instructions and other floor covering ideas.)

Unattractive Paneling

If you're up for it and your landlords permits it, you can paint paneling for a fresh new look. Be sure to use a primer first and to use a paint specifically formulated for paneling. Wallpaper is another alternative, but it can be costlier and more time-consuming than painting. And if your paneling has any grooves, it could be tricky to get it smooth.

For a more temporary cover-up, try painting or wallpapering several pieces of wood and hinging them together to create a screen. Place the screen in front of a paneled wall to distract from it. Old doors can also be hinged together to create a screen for the same use.

No Moldings

You can paint on your own molding by trimming your windows and doors in a neutral paint color. Make your "faux molding" a few inches wide. If you're a little more daring or artistic, try using a stencil design for a more unique painted-on molding.

Size of Space

Space Is Small

Small spaces don't require small furnishings! A large piece or two can actually distract from a room's small size and help it appear less compact. Also go for smart, multipurpose pieces, such as those mentioned in chapter 9. You may also want to keep the room light and airy so it won't feel so closed in.

Space Is Too Large

Create "nooks" or "activity centers" within a larger room to make it seem less vast and a bit more comfortable to spend time in. Designate the nooks with area rugs, paint colors, or furniture positioning.

Painting Tips

You've decided to paint, and you're itching to get started. Painting is a relatively simple and inexpensive way to transform your space. But beginning the job and realizing you don't have what you need or didn't plan well can be frustrating. To avoid that frustration, check out the following painting tips:

Get Ready . . .

Measure your rooms and take those measurements to a paint store. The staff there will be able to figure out how many gallons you'll need to do the job. If you're really cautious about a particular color, try this: have the store mix up a small can of the color you've chosen. Take it home and test it out on a small section of wall before you commit an entire room.

Materials

Paint

Rollers

Brushes

Edger

Tape

Dropcloths

Screwdriver

Spackle and spackling tool

Get Set . . .

1. Clean all surfaces to be painted (at least remove dust or cobwebs that may be present).

2. Repair damaged areas.

3. Remove hardware, such as light switch plates.

4. Remove window treatments.

5. Remove all artwork and other items from the walls.

6. Remove nails or screws from the walls.

7. Fill in holes with Spackle.

8. Move furniture away from the walls.

9. Place dropcloths on furniture and floors.

10. Open windows to assure proper ventilation.

11. Dress in clothing that you won't mind getting splattered with paint.

Go!

1. Don't rush! Take your time and do the job right and you won't have to redo it later. Recruit help if you need it from family and friends.

2. Take breaks so you can stretch, drink, and eat. It's important to keep your energy up while you work.

3. Tape off all moldings (or use an edger) so your paint won't end up in the wrong places.

4. If you're painting a light color over a dark color, cover the surface with a primer first. Allow the primer to dry, and then paint on the color of your choice.

5. Paint in light, even strokes until you have the coverage you desire.

6. Clean drips as you go.

7. Enjoy your new room!

Flea Market/
Yard Sale Planner

Are you ready to head out for an exciting day of flea market and yard sale shopping? Wait–don't head out yet. Shopping flea markets and yard sales is quite different from hitting the local mall in search of goods. You may have to dig through quite a lot of junk in search for the perfect decorating gem, so you'll want to be sure you're dressed and equipped for whatever the day may bring.

What to Wear

Comfortable shoes

Clothing that can get soiled

Sunglasses and a hat or cap

Sunscreen

A fanny pack (The kind that attaches with a belt to your waist. It makes for easy access to cash.)

What to Bring

Raincoat

Umbrella

Cash (lots of small bills)

Flashlight

Magnifying glass

Bagged snack and lunch, small cooler with drinks and ice

A Thermos full of coffee or tea for cold days

Gloves

Rolling cart

Large shopping bag

Towels and newspaper (for wrapping breakables)

The Game Plan

Get out as early as possible, but *after* a good breakfast.

Print out maps from an Internet mapping tool (or use an old-fashioned city map), and plan your route efficiently.

Don't be afraid to negotiate.

Ask for additional discounts when you're purchasing several things from the same vendor.

If you see something you love, don't leave without it. (It probably won't be there later.)

Take along a friend to use as a sounding board.

Move Planner

So you've found a great new apartment and you're ready to throw your things into some boxes and move right in? Wait! Why not create an organized plan for your move, to help make it less painful? Let's face it, moving isn't always the most pleasant of experiences. So try the tips listed here to help you organize your move and make it go more smoothly.

Several Months Before the Move

- Locate an apartment.

- Take apartment measurements if possible—be sure to measure doorways and windows (for window treatments), as well as entire room dimensions.

- Create a plan to organize your current belongings. Make your priority list and begin setting aside time each week to sift through and purge your unwanted belongings.

- Create a list of the items you'd like to purchase, and keep that list with you at all times.

- Begin visiting stores, flea markets, yard sales, and Web sites to search for the items you want.

- Begin obtaining moving company quotes or recruiting friends and family members to help on moving day.

One Month Before the Move

⊚ Begin collecting boxes and other packing materials. (Be sure to check with friends who moved recently.)

⊚ Begin packing items you won't need during the next month, such as off-season clothing and personal papers. Clearly label all boxes with the contents and the room where they will be used. You can also take an instant photograph of box contents (group them all together on the floor before you place them in the box) and tape it to the outside of the box.

⊚ Set up utilities for your new apartment; arrange for cancellation (or switching over) of utilities for your current home. Be sure to have the utilities in your new place activated the day before you move in, if possible. This will help assure that you'll have them up and running whenever you arrive.

⊚ Obtain a change-of-address kit from your local post office. Also purchase (or make) personal new-address notes to distribute.

One to Two Weeks Before the Move

✣ On grid paper, draw out your new apartment rooms and experiment with furniture placement.

✣ Complete your furniture and accessory inventory (located in this section).

✣ Create a "first day" box. It should contain some clothing, a set of linens, a towel, toiletries, medications, a few snacks, and other items you don't want to have to search for on your first day, in case your unpacking isn't complete before bedtime. Also include a list of necessary phone numbers, such as utility companies.

❖ Clean out your refrigerator, oven, closets, and other areas of your current apartment.

❖ Have your carpeting steam cleaned, if you choose to or if your landlord requires it.

❖ Fix any holes you may have left in the walls.

❖ Charge up your cellular phone.

❖ Mail your personal change-of-address cards to family, friends, and associates.

❖ Complete your packing, other than the items you will use for the next week or two. Label and number your boxes.

Moving Day

⊚ Take all valuables, such as jewelry, with you in your car (or however your will travel to your new apartment)—do not pack them in boxes and load them onto a moving van. The same goes for computers, which can be damaged during a move if they knock around in a truck or moving van.

⊚ Turn in your keys for the apartment you are exiting.

⊚ Arrive at your new apartment before the movers, so you can open doors, test appliances, and verify that all utilities are on.

⊚ Verify that the appropriate number of boxes arrive at your new place.

⊚ Notify your landlord of any problems, such as appliances that aren't working properly.

Entertainment Planner

Whether you're hosting a casual dinner party, a birthday bash, or a New Year's Eve extravaganza, you'll want to dress up your apartment so it looks special for the occasion. To prepare for and decorate for special events, try the following tips:

- **Two to four weeks before the party.** Decide on a date, location, time, and theme for the party. Begin to plan the menu. (Try Internet sites like Cooking.com for great recipe ideas.)

- **One to two weeks before the party.** Send out invitations with all the specifics, such as the time, dress, and whether an RSVP is needed. Be sure to include a map to your place, if necessary.

- **One week before the party.** Make final decisions on the menu, organize recipes, and purchase the necessary ingredients. Purchase or work on decorations, such as candles, streamers, and balloons. Also shop around for items such as paper products. If guests are calling to ask what they can bring, assign some menu items (e.g., appetizers, dessert, or drinks) so you can cross them off your list.

- **One day before the party.** Begin food preparation. Precook any food that will keep well overnight and thaw out foods that are frozen (e.g., meats) in the refrigerator. Clean your apartment thoroughly, especially areas guests will use, such as bathrooms. Begin to hang up or set out decorations. Select music to be played. Clean and set out all trays and servers you plan to use tomorrow.

❖ **Party day.** Give yourself plenty of time, and don't forget to include the time you'll need to prepare yourself! Recruit help if you can. Lay out extra hand towels, toilet paper, and soaps, so guests won't have to go looking for these items. Complete your decorating, vacuum your floors, light some candles, get the food preparations started, and let the party begin!

Accessory Inventory

It's difficult to determine the accessories you need until you have a good handle on what you already have. Using this inventory sheet, go from room to room, noting your accessories and their current condition. This exercise may even give you ideas for different uses of your accessories in different rooms. It will also help you assure that all your belongings are accounted for after a move.

Living Room

Item	Condition	Replacement Needed?

Kitchen

Item	Condition	Replacement Needed?

Bedroom

Item	Condition	Replacement Needed?

Bathroom

Item	Condition	Replacement Needed?

Other Room: _____

Item	Condition	Replacement Needed?

Furniture Inventory

Like the accessory inventory sheet, this sheet will help you examine exactly what furniture you have, what you should replace, and what you may need to purchase.

Living Room

Item	Condition	Replacement Needed?

Kitchen

Item	Condition	Replacement Needed?

Bedroom

Item	Condition	Replacement Needed?

Bathroom

Item	Condition	Replacement Needed?
_____	_____	_____
_____	_____	_____
_____	_____	_____
_____	_____	_____
_____	_____	_____
_____	_____	_____
_____	_____	_____
_____	_____	_____
_____	_____	_____

Other Room: _____

Item	Condition	Replacement Needed?
_____	_____	_____
_____	_____	_____
_____	_____	_____
_____	_____	_____
_____	_____	_____
_____	_____	_____
_____	_____	_____
_____	_____	_____
_____	_____	_____

Index

About the Author

Lourdes Dumke is a lifestyle writer specializing in decorating articles. She was introduced to flea market and budget shopping by her parents while she was growing up in south Florida. Twenty years later, she reclaimed her interest in "junk" that was born in the hot, dusty swap meets she visited as a child. She now shares her decorating ideas and adventures with the world through her writing.

Dumke graduated from the University of Florida in 1986 with a degree in journalism. Over the past fifteen years, she has worked as a magazine editor, corporate communications manager, and freelance writer.

In 1999, she became the budget decorating contributing editor for Suite101.com–a large, Internet-based community where hosts write articles and lead forums dedicated to more than a thousand topics. Her decorating and lifestyle articles have been widely published over the past few years.

Dumke spends most of her weekends hunting for decorating bargains and used treasures to recycle. She lives in northern Georgia with her husband and two children.

photo by Tim Glover

279

Master the Art of Keeping House—the Easy Way!

This lifesaver of a book provides all the essential secrets, basic instructions, and creative tricks on the best ways to keep house, from laundry and housecleaning to floor and carpet care and minor home repairs. Whether you are single, married, a home owner or apartment dweller, you will discover how to efficiently take care of your home, as well as yourself! Mom's favorite housekeeping secrets include:

- How to clean, room-by-room
- Must-have supplies and how to make your own
- The proper care of floors, carpets, and furniture
- How to clean when you only have an hour
- And many more!

ISBN 0-7615-2819-9 / Paperback
272 pages / U.S. $16.95 / Can. $25.95

Available everywhere books are sold.
Visit us online at www.primapublishing.com.

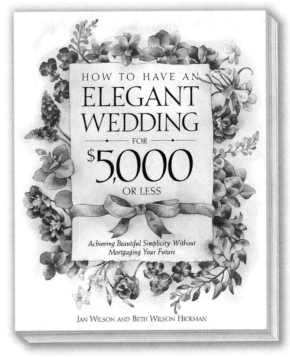

To Order Books

Please send me the following items:

Quantity	Title	Unit Price	Total
_____	_____	$ _____	$ _____
_____	_____	$ _____	$ _____
_____	_____	$ _____	$ _____
_____	_____	$ _____	$ _____
_____	_____	$ _____	$ _____
_____	_____	$ _____	$ _____
_____	_____	$ _____	$ _____
_____	_____	$ _____	$ _____

Subtotal $ _____
7% Sales Tax (CA only) $ _____
7% Sales Tax (PA only) $ _____
5% Sales Tax (IN only) $ _____
7% G.S.T. Tax (Canada only) $ _____
Priority Shipping $ _____
Total Order $ _____

By Telephone: With American Express, MC, or Visa,
call 800-632-8676, Monday–Friday, 8:30–4:30
www.primapublishing.com

By E-mail: sales@primapub.com

By Mail: Just fill out the information below and send with your remittance to:
Prima Publishing ▪ 3000 Lava Ridge Court ▪ Roseville, CA 95661

Name _____

Address _____

City _____ State _____ ZIP _____

MC/Visa/American Express# _____ Exp. _____

Check/money order enclosed for $ _____ Payable to Prima Publishing

Daytime telephone _____

Signature _____

**Indianapolis
Marion County
Public Library**

**Renew by Phone
269-5222**

Renew on the Web
www.imcpl.org

For General Library Information
please call 269-1700